500 KEY WORDS FOR THE SAT*

AND HOW TO REMEMBER THEM FOREVER!

Charles Gulotta

Illustrated by Trish Dardine

Published by
Mostly Bright Ideas

*SAT is a registered trademark of the College Entrance Examination Board, which does not endorse this product.

This is the twelfth edition.

ISBN-10: 0-9653263-3-0
ISBN-13: 978-0-96532-633-9

Contents

Introduction
page 4

The 500 words
page 8

The 135 words that didn't make it
page 113

SAT Critical Reading: How to Avoid the Traps
page 116

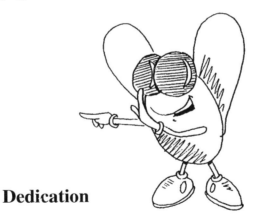

Dedication

This book is dedicated to everyone who's ever gone blank while taking a test, or said "profane" when they meant "profound," or wished they'd studied Latin when they had the chance. But most of all, it's dedicated to those of you who believe you just aren't smart enough to learn. Because you certainly are.

Introduction

The 2009 edition.

We first published *500 SAT Words, and How to Remember Them Forever!* in 1992, which means it's been in print continually for seventeen years. During that time, we've sold more than eighty thousand copies. Not exactly a bestseller, but satisfying nevertheless, because it means a few people have found the book useful. And while we've been reluctant to make major changes, each edition has been slightly different from the ones that came before. In the 2002 version, we changed the title to *500 Key Words for the SAT, and How to Remember Them Forever!* Over the years, many readers had suggested that we include sample sentences for each of the five hundred words. We eventually followed their advice. Other than that, it's basically the same book we've been publishing since 1992.

The purpose of this book

This book exists because there are a bunch of words you need to know. You'll find five hundred of them on the pages that follow.

If learning vocabulary words doesn't seem like a big thrill, try to see the whole picture. It isn't, I admit, as much fun as a cruise ship stocked with jelly doughnuts. At the same time, it's much better than being pushed off a cliff into a dark, rat-infested swamp. Or having abdominal surgery. Or watching bowling on television.

Now that we have things in perspective, let's get to work. But wait a minute, you're thinking. Five hundred words! That's a big number. How will I ever have time to take care of my basic physical requirements, not to mention maintain contact with my family, if I have to learn five hundred words?

Five hundred may seem like a lot, but it really isn't. You can learn all of these words with very little effort. Your brain is capable of absorbing, understanding, and storing millions of facts and ideas. Just think about how many songs you know, how many famous faces you recognize, how many thoughts and memories and images and sounds and voices you can see and hear in your head. Think about how many different kinds of breakfast cereal you can name. Learning five hundred new words should be easy. And it is.

But wait another minute, you're thinking. These aren't just any five hundred words. These are five hundred hard words. These are five hundred of the words I've been trying to avoid. Well, here's the good news: there *are* no hard words in this book.

There are no hard words on the SAT either. Really, there aren't.

What makes a word hard or easy? Is it the number of letters? The number of syllables? No, you know many words with ten or more letters. You know many words with five or more syllables. And you'd have no trouble defining those words. At the same time, there are short words, some just three or four letters, that neither you nor I could begin to define or explain.

The words that are hard, truly hard, are the ones that have hard-to-understand meanings. Like "erg," for example, a common physics term. Here's the definition of erg as it appears in *Webster's Third New International Dictionary*: "An absolute cgs unit of work representing the work done by a force of one dyne acting through a displacement of one centimeter in the direction of the force." (Notice, by the way, that erg has just three letters and one syllable.)

So what's so special about the five hundred words in this book? A few things. For one, they appear frequently on the SAT and other tests. They also tend to show up in college courses. Depending on what you read and who you hang around with, it's likely they will continue to show up for the rest of your life. These are the words that comprise much of the language of educated adulthood.

Does that make them hard? No. Again, these words are not hard. They're just *unfamiliar*. And that's certainly no cause for despair because every word you know now was, at one time, unfamiliar. (At some point in your life, "helicopter" was a hard word.) Once you get acquainted with a word, once it becomes familiar, it loses its mystery and its power to confuse or frighten you. Eventually it becomes an old friend, one of the easy words.

Here's more good news

Almost without exception, the unfamiliar word turns out to have a simple meaning. Look quickly through this book and notice the meanings of the words. You'll find definitions like "big," "small," "fast," "poor," "greedy," and "quiet." There's just nothing difficult about what these words are trying to say to you.

So what *is* the difficult part? It's this: when you try to remember what these unfamiliar words mean, you have trouble even though their meanings are simple. Why? Because they're not part of your everyday speech and writing. You don't see these words, you don't hear them, and you don't use them. So you've had no reason to remember them.

Until now, that is.

You're looking at this book, so you must have some purpose for wanting to build your vocabulary. Maybe you're preparing for one of the standardized tests. Maybe you want to improve your grades in English class. Or maybe you're just looking to increase your command of the language. Whatever your goal, I believe this book will help you reach it, and quickly.

How it all works

For each of the five hundred words, we're going to start with the unfamiliar word and its simple meaning, and we're going to create a bridge between them. The bridge will be in the form of a picture. This picture is like the missing piece of a jigsaw puzzle. It fits the word perfectly on one end and the meaning on the other. Set it in place and your path from word to meaning is clear.

Let's take a look at one example: the word "avarice."

"Avarice" means "greed." Let's create a picture that helps you connect them. We'll do that by breaking the word avarice in half: Ava rice. Picture a woman named Ava seated at a table, a mound of rice piled in front of her. Ava has her arms around the rice because she doesn't want anyone else to get any. So *Ava*, with the *rice*, is demonstrating *greed*. Concentrate on this picture for a few seconds, together with the idea of greed, and burn the image into your memory. From now on, whenever you see or hear the word avarice, think of Ava and her rice and remember how greedy she is. It's as simple as that.

In some cases, we'll break the word apart, as we just did with "avarice." In others, we'll use a word or phrase that looks or sounds like the word we're learning (for example, "celerity" looks like "celery"). Occasionally we'll use the more common meaning of a word to learn its secondary definition ("wax" as a verb means to grow larger, so we'll picture a ball of wax getting bigger). Approximately one hundred of the words are illustrated with cartoons.

In all cases, as you'll notice, the pictures are bizarre and ridiculous. This will help you remember them. The stranger the image, the easier it is to recall. Now find the following entry on page 17:

AVARICE (AH-ver-iss) *noun* — **greed**

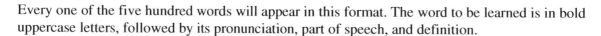

Looks like: Ava rice

Picture: A woman named Ava seated at a table with her arms around a mound of rice; she won't share the rice with anyone. She's greedy.

Other form: Avaricious *(adj)*

Sentence: Success can lead to either great generosity or *avarice*.

Every one of the five hundred words will appear in this format. The word to be learned is in bold uppercase letters, followed by its pronunciation, part of speech, and definition.

The next line suggests a cue, based on what the word looks or sounds like. In the example, the cue for "avarice" was "Ava rice." This cue will help you recall a picture, which will immediately lead you to the word's meaning. (If this sounds like too much work, just try a few and you'll see that it isn't. You will remember the cues, pictures, and meanings quickly and on a long-term basis.)

The next line describes the picture or tells a story that illustrates the word and its meaning. A few of these stories are longer than you might expect, but again, you don't have to memorize them. All you need to take away from each entry is the definition and the image that will help you remember it.

The phrase "Other form" presents the word you're learning as it appears in other parts of speech. So when you learn "avarice" as a noun you'll also learn "avaricious" as an adjective. With many of the words you'll also find a "Note" at the bottom of the entry. These notes tell you to make a mental connection with other words, or warn you about being confused by a similar-looking word. Sometimes the note will point out the root of the word and suggest other words with the same root.

Check out these related words in the dictionary to further build your vocabulary.

Finally, each entry ends with the word used in a sentence.

Just a quick comment on pronunciation. I've avoided using the dictionary method of explaining how to pronounce a word, mostly because the dictionary uses weird stuff like upside-down "e"s and dots over letters and I find those things confusing. I've spelled out the pronunciations, with the accented syllables in uppercase, based on the way I say the words. I mention this because we're often creating pictures based on what the words *sound* like. Your pronunciation may be slightly different.

At the end of this book you'll find a list of words that should have been included but weren't, either because there was no more room or because I couldn't think of a picture. They are just as important as the five hundred in the main part of the book, and you should make a point of learning them. Beginning on page 116, you'll also find some helpful hints for approaching the SAT's Critical Reading section. You'll learn about some of the many sources of confusion in the English language -- such as look-alike and sound-alike words -- how the testmakers take advantage of that confusion, and how you can avoid falling into the traps they've set for you on the SAT.

So what now?

That's up to you. How much and how quickly do you want to learn? I've used this technique to help students learn as many as thirty words in an hour. However, five at a time seems to be a comfortable number for most people. It might help to write the words down as you learn them, along with short, one or two-word definitions. If some words give you trouble, include a description of the picture for those words. For example: "Avarice -- greed -- Ava and her rice." As you add to your list, look over the words you've already learned. You may find that after reviewing a word two or three times, you no longer need the picture. You'll just come up with the definition, as if you've always known it.

A special note to younger students

You may not be familiar with the SAT yet, but in a few years it will suddenly become very important. If you're already working with this book, you're off to a great start. Keep learning new words wherever and whenever you can. The ability to do so is a skill that will help you a great deal on the SAT -- and for the rest of your life.

Read, read, read!

Remembering the meaning of a word is only the first step. This may sound strange, but try to get acquainted with each word. Learn how to spell it, and how to recognize its other forms. Notice how it's used in books and newspapers. Then, gradually, work the word into your writing and speech. Eventually it will become a natural part of your language. That's when you've truly learned it.

Building a strong vocabulary is a lifelong process. I hope this book helps to make it a little easier, and a little more fun.

Charles Setter

ABSTRACT (ab-STRAHKT) *adj* — theoretical; not concrete

Think of: absent tracks

Picture: A steam train riding on invisible tracks. The tracks are abstract, just an idea.

Other form: Abstraction *(noun)*

Sentence: Advanced algebra is too *abstract* for most people.

IT'S FROM THE ABB BROTHERS... A TRUCE I THINK, BUT I DON'T UNDERSTAND IT.

ABSTRUSE (ab-STROOSE) *adj* — hard to understand

Sounds like: Abb's truce

Picture: A hillbilly holding a rifle in one hand and a note in the other. The note may be a truce from the family he's been feuding with (the Abbs), but he's not sure because it's hard to understand.

Other forms: Abstrusely *(adv)*; abstruseness *(noun)*

Sentence: Her *abstruse* explanation of the accident was bewildering.

ACCLAIM (uh-CLAME) *verb* — praise; applaud

Sounds like: a claim

Picture: An insurance company. The newcomer on the staff has just handled her first claim. Her co-workers, a supportive bunch, are all clapping for her and offering their congratulations.

Other forms: Acclaim, acclamation *(nouns)* (Don't confuse with "acclimation.")

Sentence: Mark Twain was a highly-*acclaimed* author and lecturer.

ACCOLADE (AKK-oh-lade) *noun* — an award, or praise

Sounds like: echo lad

Picture: A young boy is standing on the edge of a cliff, facing a vertical wall of rock. He yells wonderful things about himself so that his voice echoes off the wall and comes back to him.

Sentence: The film received *accolades* from both the critics and the general public.

ACQUIESCENT (ak-wee-ESS-ent) *adj* — reluctantly agreeable; compliant

Sounds like: agree yes cent

First: Go to COMPLACENT and get that picture in your mind, then come back here.

Picture: The same penny seated on the bench. The children urge the penny to play with them. He knows they will never give up, so he gives in and quietly and reluctantly gets up to play.

Other forms: Acquiesce *(verb)*; acquiescence *(noun)*

8   Sentence: Some employers insist on *acquiescence* and will fire anyone who rebels.

ACRIMONY (AK-rih-mo-nee) *noun* — **words or behavior filled with harshness or anger**

Looks like: acre money

Picture: Two neighboring farmers arguing over who owns a certain acre of land.
Farmer 1: "This is my acre. You want it? Give me my money and it's yours!"
Farmer 2: "Your money? This is my land, you big, ugly, stupid farmer. Now get out of here before I say something *really* acrimonious!"

Other forms: Acrimonious *(adj);* acrimoniously *(adv)*

Sentence: Unfortunately, divorce proceedings are often filled with *acrimony*.

ADAMANT (ADD-um-ent) *adj* — **refusing to change; stubborn, unyielding**

Looks like: a dam ant

Picture: A giant ant acting as a dam, blocking a stream. The other ants need the water for their colony. "Come on," they say, "get out of the way!" But the large ant refuses to move.

Sentence: She was *adamant* that her son be home by midnight.

ADROIT (uh-DROYT) *adj* — **skillful in physical activity, or in handling difficult situations**

Looks like: android, which is a human-like robot

Picture: An android playing basketball. He dribbles behind his back and does reverse lay-ups with either hand. A reporter is impressed: "He has the best skills I've ever seen. And he's equally adroit at handling the media, particularly concerning his use of illegal battery packs in the Olympics."

Sentence: Her *adroitness* on the balance beam stunned the crowd.

ADVOCATE (AD-vuh-kate) *verb* — **support; plead for; speak on behalf of**

Sounds like: ad for Kate

Picture: Kate is seeking her first job. She's smart and well-educated, but has no experience. Kate's aunt, publisher of the local newspaper, has always encouraged Kate. She begins running ads, telling the reader how talented and reliable Kate is. "I strongly advocate your hiring her" says each ad.

Other forms: Advocate, advocacy *(nouns)*

Sentence: Lawyers *advocate* for their clients.

AFFABLE (AFF-uh-bull) *adj* — **friendly; easygoing**

Looks like: a fable

Think of: Aesop's Fables. Picture Aesop, a Greek man who lived about 500 B.C. Imagine him as a friendly, outgoing person, standing in the center of the village and greeting people as they pass by.

Other forms: Affability *(noun);* affably *(adv)*

Sentence: Most television news anchors appear to be *affable*, at least on the air.

AFFIRMATION (aff-er-MAY-shun) *noun* — **positive statement; assertion; agreement**

Confirm

Sounds like: a firm Asian

Picture: A muscular man from the Orient being interviewed by a TV news reporter. "We've heard," says the reporter, "that you plan to break the world weightlifting record by lifting a Toyota filled with Sumo wrestlers. Is this true?" "Yes," replies the Asian man. "And that includes a full tank of gas and maps in the glove compartment." Looking into the TV camera, the reporter says, "Up until now it had been just another unfounded rumor. But now we've received affirmation."

Other forms: Affirm *(verb);* affirmative *(adj);* affirmatively *(adv)*

Sentence: The prime minister saw her re-election as an *affirmation* of her policies.

ALIENATE (AIL-ee-uh-nate) *verb* — **to push someone away, or cause him to separate from people**

Sounds like: Alien Nate

Picture: Nate, a Martian, is standing apart from a group of former Earthling friends. One says, "We don't want him around anymore. He's weird. It's like he's from another planet or something."

Other forms: Alien, alienation *(nouns)*

Sentence: People who think they know everything often *alienate* their friends.

ALOOF (uh-LOOF) *adj* — **detached; apart; indifferent**

Sounds like: a roof

Picture: Person on the roof of a house, refusing to even look at the people below. He has completely removed himself from the group.

Sentence: He always sat alone, so people assumed he was *aloof.*

ALTRUISTIC (al-troo-ISS-tik) *adj* — **unselfish; caring**

Sounds like: Al True's Wish Stick

Picture: A man named Al True has a "wish stick," or magic wand. He uses it to help people by giving them what they need.   Other form: Altruism *(noun)*

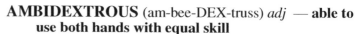

Sentence: Most religions teach that *altruism* is good.

AMBIDEXTROUS (am-bee-DEX-truss) *adj* — **able to use both hands with equal skill**

Sounds like: Bambi Dextrous

Picture: A baseball pitcher named Bambi Dextrous who pitches with both hands at the same time.

Sentence: Juggling must be easier for people who are *ambidextrous.*   Connect with: Dexterity

AMBIGUOUS (am-BIG-yoo-uss) *adj* — **unclear; vague; having several possible interpretations**

Sounds like: a big U.S.

Picture: Mother and son are standing at the front door. Son is about to leave on a trip.
Mom: So where exactly are you going?
Son: Somewhere.
Mom: Somewhere where?
Son: Somewhere in the U.S.
Mom: You're being very vague. It's a big U.S. out there.

Other forms: Ambiguity *(noun);* ambiguously *(adv)*

Sentence: When questioned by police, the suspect gave *ambiguous* answers.

AMBIVALENCE (am-BIV-uh-lence) *noun* — **indecision; feeling of being pulled in two directions**

Looks like: Val inside ambulance (ambiVALence)

Picture: Val is about to have a baby. She's gone into labor while her husband is at work. She's called for an ambulance to take her to the hospital, but now that she's inside the ambulance she's having second thoughts about going without her husband: "Wait! Let's give him a few more minutes. No, we should go. I'm in labor. Okay, take me to the hospital. No, wait! Maybe he'll get here soon..."

Other forms: Ambivalent *(adj);* ambivalently *(adv)*

Sentence: The house had been in the family for generations, so they were *ambivalent* about selling it.

AMELIORATE (uh-MEEL-ee-or-ate) *verb* — **to make an unpleasant situation better; to improve**

Sounds like: a meteor ate

Picture: A house was overrun with two-headed snakes. Suddenly, a meteor swooped down and gobbled up all the snakes. So a meteor ate the snakes and improved the situation in the house.

Sentence: The terrible working conditions were *ameliorated* only by her friendly co-workers.

AMITY (AM-ih-tee) *noun* — **friendship**

Sounds like: Emma tea

Picture: A lady named Emma who invites neighbors and passersby over to her house for tea every day. Visitors are lined up at the front door, while a steady stream of people holding teacups flows from the back door and spills out onto the back lawn. A smiling Emma says, "I'm just trying to be friendly."

Connect with: Amicable *(adj)*, amigo *(Spanish)*

Sentence: Complete *amity* among bordering nations is always difficult.

AMORPHOUS (ay-MORF-uss) *adj* — **without form or shape**

Sounds like: "Yay, more for us!"

Picture: A mother bringing her three children bowls of some shapeless food. One of the kids says, "Yay, more for us!" One of the others says, "Yeah, but more what?"

Sentence: Liquid water is *amorphous*; it always takes on the shape of its container.

Connect with: Metamorphosis

ANALOGOUS (uh-NAHL-uh-guss) *adj* — **similar**

Sounds like: an alligator

Picture: Two alligators that look exactly alike.

Other form: Analogy *(noun)*

Sentence: A camera's aperture is *analogous* to the pupil of the eye.

ANARCHY (AN-arr-kee) *noun* — **a lack of order; chaos**

Sounds like: an ark key

Picture: The animals on Noah's Ark are running wild. Noah, standing on the pier, has somehow been locked out. He's yelling, "My key! Please, someone give me an ark key! This is chaos!"

Other form: Anarchist *(noun)*

Sentence: Without laws and rules, there would be *anarchy* everywhere.

ANATHEMA (uh-NATH-a-ma) *noun* — **a religious curse, or the thing or person being cursed**

Looks like: an anthem

Picture: A man who, many years ago, fled his native country because of the cruel government in power there. Now, as an old man, he finds a record in his attic. When he plays the record, he hears, for the first time in four decades, the national anthem of his former home. The song reminds him of the cruel dictator still in power and he spits on the record, cursing the words, the dictator, and the entire government. The anthem is now anathema to him.

Sentence: For many people in India, the killing of cows is *anathema*.

ANTAGONISTIC (an-tag-uh-NISS-tik) *adj* — **in hostile competition; opposing**

Sounds like: ant tag on his stick

Picture: An ant holding a stick; on the stick hangs a tag that says, "I'll fight anybody, any time. How about right now?"

Other forms: Antagonist, antagonism *(nouns)*; antagonize *(verb)*

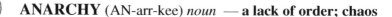

Sentence: Political parties are often *antagonistic* toward each other.

ANTIQUATED (ANN-tih-quay-ted) *adj* — **too old to be useful; outdated; obsolete**

Sounds like: Auntie Katie

Picture: A very, very old woman named Auntie Katie. She lives in an old house with an old dog and old furniture. Every single thing in Auntie Katie's life is antiquated.

Connect with: Antique, antiquity *(nouns)*

Sentence: The wiring in some old houses is too *antiquated* to handle modern appliances.

ANTITHESIS (ann-TITH-ih-sis) *noun* — **opposite**

Sounds like: anTEETHesis

Picture: The teeth in your mouth. For every tooth, there is an opposite tooth. For example, for every upper tooth, there is a corresponding (opposite) lower tooth.

Other form: Antithetical *(adj)*

Sentence: Ignorance is the *antithesis* of knowledge.

APATHY (APP-uh-thee) *noun* — **lack of interest or concern**

Sounds like: apple tree

Picture: George Washington's father is questioning him about the cherry tree that has been chopped down. Young George, arms folded, replies: "I cannot tell a lie. I really don't care who chopped down the cherry tree."

Other form: Apathetic *(adj)*

Sentence: Many citizens are *apathetic* about elections and don't bother to vote.

APEX (AY-pex) *noun* — **top; highest point; summit**

Looks like: ape x

Picture: King Kong (the ape) climbing the Empire State Building. He's trying to get to a large letter "X" which is perched on top of the building's antenna (the highest point). As he climbs, he thinks to himself, "This will be the apex of my career."

Sentence: It took the mountain-climbers four days to reach the *apex*.

APPEASE (uh-PEEZ) *verb* — **calm; pacify**

Sounds like: peas

Picture: A young child who's upset because he's hungry. He calms down when his mother gives him some peas (this requires a little extra imagination). Or, just think of "please" or "a peace," all of which sound like appease and suggest its meaning.

Other form: Appeasement *(noun)*

Sentence: Management tried to *appease* the strikers with a small salary increase.

ARBITRARY (ARR-bih-treh-ree) *adj* — **selected by random choice and without solid reason**

Sounds like: our bee, Jerry

Picture: A giant glass tank called the Lost Bee Shelter. A young man is looking into the tank at thousands of flying bees. He says to the attendant, "I think that's him. That's our bee, Jerry."

Other form: Arbitrarily *(adv)*

Sentence: Your selection of a seat in a nearly empty theater is somewhat *arbitrary*.

13

ARCANE (ar-KANE) *adj* — **secret; mysterious**

Sounds like: our cane

Picture: A child sits at his grandparents' dinner table. In the corner of the room is a wooden cane with strange words and markings on it. When the boy asks what it all means, his grandmother says mysteriously, "Oh, that's just our cane. Don't worry about it. You wouldn't understand anyway."

Sentence: The walls of the pyramid were covered with *arcane* symbols.

ARCHAIC (arr-KAY-ik) *adj* — **old; antiquated**

Sounds like: our cake

Picture: A very old cake, covered with cobwebs. One person asks, "Where did we get our cake?" The other person answers, "From Auntie Katie, where else?" (See ANTIQUATED.)

Sentence: Many words and expressions used in the nineteenth century seem *archaic* to us now.

ARROGANT (AHR-oh-gint) *adj* — **acting superior, obnoxious, smug, or rude**

Looks like: arrow can't

Picture: It's the mid-1800s, somewhere in Oklahoma. A rifle salesman is making a presentation to some Navaho Indians. "You're still using those bows and arrows for hunting?" he asks. "This rifle fires bullets. Do you people know what bullets are?" The Navaho look at each other, annoyed but patient. The salesman continues: "A bullet can take down a buffalo from five hundred yards. An arrow can't! A bullet can fly faster than a hawk. An arrow can't! And a bullet can be kept in your pocket or pouch. An arrow can't! You have to buy my rifles and bullets, because they're better than anything you're using."

Other forms: Arrogance *(noun)*; arrogantly *(adv)*

Sentence: The trick is to be self-confident without being *arrogant*.

ARTICULATE (ar-TICK-u-let) *adj* — **able to speak clearly and effectively**

Looks like: Artie Kool-Aid

Picture: A man named Artie holding a pitcher, giving a speech: "...and let me assure you, dear fellows, that it would be a veritable impossibility for me to be so eloquent without this extraordinary thirst-quenching concoction, Kool-Aid."

Other forms: Articulation *(noun)*, articulate *(verb)*

Sentence: To be effective, a preacher must be *articulate*.

ASCENDANCE (uh-SEN-dence) *noun* — **domination; controlling power**

Sounds like: a sun dance

Picture: This Indian tribe has been doing rain dances for many centuries. But now it's been raining for seven weeks and they need the sun to dry up the water. So they create and perform a sun dance. After the dancers have been performing for several minutes, the clouds disappear and the sun comes out. The tribe, at least on this occasion, seems to have gained ascendance over the sun.

Other forms: Ascendant *(adj)*; ascendancy *(noun)*

Sentence: The dictator's *ascendance* to power was sudden and unstoppable.

ASCETIC (uh-SET-ik) *noun* — **person who rejects physical comfort and luxury for self-discipline**

Sounds like: acidic (containing a high level of acid)

Picture: A man of great religious faith has decided to leave his comfortable life behind in order to reach a higher level of spiritual growth. He gives away all of his possessions, including his house, donates his savings to charity, and begins to walk across the desert. Many days later, his shoes worn through and his clothes in tatters, he reaches the end of the desert and finds himself at a gas station. A mechanic, recognizing the religious man's obvious need for a drink, offers him a cold can from the vending machine. However, the man sees the soft drink as a luxury, an aspect of the physical world no longer part of his life, and rejects it, choosing instead to drink from a nearby bucket of battery acid. Surprised, the mechanic says, "Why, that's downright acidic!" "I think you mean 'ascetic,'" says the religious man, between sips.

Other forms: Ascetic (adj); asceticism *(noun)*; ascetically *(adv)*

Sentence: Some religious leaders of the past believed the life of an *ascetic* led to spiritual growth.

ASPERITY (uh-SPERR-ih-tee) *adj* — **roughness; harshness; irritability**

Sounds like: a spirit tea

Picture: A group of ghosts (spirits) meeting for their afternoon tea. One of the spirits gets extremely agitated and angry after drinking his tea, and begins yelling at his companions. (One of the other ghosts comments: "He really needs to start drinking decaffeinated. This regular stuff just haunts him.")

Connect with: Aspersion *(noun)* — a defaming remark

Sentence: No matter how comfortable, everyone encounters *asperity* at some time.

ASSAIL (uh-SAIL) *verb* — **attack with words or force**

Sounds like: a sail (or, a sale)

Picture: The husband comes home with another new sail for the boat. The wife attacks: "What? You spent more money on that stupid boat? You haven't bought yourself a new shirt in six years, but the sailboat is always right in style! What excuse do you have this time?" Husband: "It was on sale."

Other forms: Assailable *(adj);* assailant *(noun)*

Sentence: The university president was *assailed* for his apparently racist remarks.

ASSIDUOUS (uh-SIJ-yoo-us) *adj* — **persistent; hard-working; diligent; attentive to detail**

Sounds like: a Sid, U.S.

Picture: A devoted worker at the post office has noticed a letter sent from overseas. The envelope is addressed simply, "Sid, U.S." The worker, determined to see that the letter is delivered to the right person, has gathered every telephone directory in the country and is carefully going through each one page-by-page, making a list of every Sid in the U.S. "A Sid, U.S.," he says. "If I'm persistent and pay close attention to detail, I'll find him. Or her."

Other forms: Assiduousness *(noun);* assiduously *(adv)*

Sentence: Re-opening an old murder case requires the investigator to be *assiduous*.

ASSUAGE (uh-SWAYJ) *verb* — **relieve; ease; pacify**

Sounds like: as wage

Picture: A fairy godmother appears to a man who is seated at a table piled high with bills. The man is obviously miserable because he has no money. The fairy offers to pay the man a salary ("as wage") for the work he's doing in paying the bills! The man is thrilled, for she has assuaged his anxiety.

Sentence: Marvin bought his wife a DVD player to *assuage* her anger over his remark about the cake.

ASTUTE (uh-STOOT) *adj* — **wise; insightfully clever; shrewd**

Sounds like: a stew

Picture: As his students prepare their dishes, the cooking teacher strolls around the kitchen, peeking into each pot and casserole. He's puzzled by the contents of one stove-top pot, but after quickly scanning the ingredients, he looks the young chef straight in the eye and says, "A stew." And of course, he's right.

Other forms: Astutely *(adv);* astuteness *(noun)*

Sentence: Carol has an *astute* business sense.

ATROPHY (AH-troh-phee) *verb* — **waste away; wither**

Looks like: a trophy

Picture: A trophy with a figure on top. The figure's arms or legs are melting. (Note: The word atrophy usually refers to the way muscles waste away when they haven't been used.)

Sentence: Within a week after the accident, his muscles had begun to *atrophy*.

AUDACIOUS (aw-DAY-shuss) *adj* — **brazen; brash; nervy**

Sounds like: all day shhh's

Picture: A librarian, referring to a boy talking at a nearby table: "'Shhhh,' I say, 'please Shhhh,' all day 'Shhhh's' and he just keeps talking. What brashness! What nerve! What audacity!" The boy turns to the librarian and says, "Shhhh! I'm trying to read!"

Other forms: Audacity *(noun);* audaciously *(adv)*

Sentence: He had the *audacity* to demand a refund on pants he'd bought two years ago.

AUGMENT (awg-MENT) *verb* — **make larger; increase**

Looks like: Aug. mint

Picture: The gardener has been trying to grow mint for months, with just a few plants to show for her hard work. Then, on August 1st, she discovers her entire backyard covered with mint. "Wow!" she says. "This Aug. mint is quite an increase from the July mint!"

Other form: Augmentation *(noun)*

Sentence: Phyllis decided to *augment* her income by taking a second job.

AUSPICIOUS (aw-SPIH-shuss) *adj* — **taking place under promising conditions; likely to succeed**

Sounds like: our space shoes

Picture: Two astronauts have just landed on the planet Neptune. Looking out the window of their spaceship, they see that they are surrounded by a frozen lake. In order to accomplish their mission, they must cross the ice and return to the spaceship quickly. One astronaut thinks it's going to be very difficult. The other pulls out two pairs of special boots fitted with large ice skate blades. "This will be easy," he says. Then, gesturing to the boots, "Our space shoes!"

Sentence: It was an *auspicious* beginning to the playoffs when the team won the first two games.

AUSTERE (aw-STEER) *adj* — **stern; plain; without luxuries**

Sounds like: our steer

Picture: A rancher giving a tour of his ranch: "And this is our steer. He lives in this simple barn, eats plain dry grass, and frowns a lot. We're not sure why."

Other forms: Austerity *(noun)*; austerely *(adv)*

Sentence: The dentist's *austere* waiting room made children even more nervous.

AVARICE (AH-ver-iss) *noun* — **greed**

Looks like: Ava rice

Picture: A woman named Ava seated at a table, her arms around a mound of rice. She won't share the rice with anyone. She's greedy.

Other form: Avaricious *(adj)*

Sentence: Success can lead to either great generosity or *avarice*.

AVERSE (uh-VERSE) *adj* — **feeling repelled; wanting to avoid**

Looks exactly like: a verse

Picture: A young boy running from the classroom, screaming: "Poetry! I can't listen to poetry! Not even a verse!"

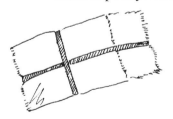

Note: Don't confuse with "adverse," which means unfavorable. Strong rains produce *adverse* conditions for golf. A golfer may be *averse* to playing in the rain.

Sentence: She was *averse* to having such a large party at her house.

HAY!

BALEFUL (BAIL-full) *adj* — **harmful; menacing**

Sounds like: bale fall

Picture: Gigantic, heavy bales of hay falling from the sky. One of the bales is about to fall onto someone.

Other form: Balefully *(adv)*

Sentence: A hungry wolf is a *baleful* sight to campers.

17

BANAL (ba-NAHL) adj
— boring; trite; insipid

Looks like: ban Al

Picture: A club's members want to keep Al from joining. "I say we ban Al," says one. "He's boring."

Other form: Banality *(noun)*

Sentence: The script was filled with *banal* and predictable scenes.

BELIE (be-LIE) *verb*
— to give an impression that is the opposite of the way things really are; to misrepresent

Looks like: bee lie

Picture: A scientist is studying the daily routines of a bumble bee, keeping careful records of what the bee does and when. Like all bees, this one is energetic and hard-working, but also like other bees, this one enjoys a good practical joke. Every day at one o'clock in the afternoon, the bee lies down on a tiny toy couch in the scientist's office and pretends to watch *All My Children*. The scientist, of course, is

surprised by the bee's behavior and notes it each day in his journal: "Every day at one, the bee lies down on the couch and watches television. Where is the industrious busy bee we've all heard about?"

Sentence: Her calm manner *belied* a fierce ambition.

BEGUILE (be-GYLE) *verb* — to cheat or deceive, usually through charm; to amuse

Sounds a little like: beg a while

Picture: Two children plotting to talk their parents into something. The older child says to the younger, "Let's try this. You go out there and beg a while. They love when you do that. They think it's cute. They'll laugh, they'll say, 'Come here and give us a hug, you cute thing,' and then they'll say yes."

Other forms: Beguiling *(adj)*; beguilingly *(adv)*

Connect with: Guile, which means deceitful shrewdness.

Sentence: At first, she was *beguiled* by his charm and attention.

BELLIGERENT (buh-LIJ-er-int) *adj* — having a strong tendency to argue and fight

Sounds like: bell ledger rent

Picture: The landlord is standing at your door, holding his rent ledger and ringing a large bell. By the time you open the door, he's rung the bell three more times. "Where's your rent?" he asks angrily, waving his ledger in the air. "It was due an hour ago. I'm going to stand here and ring this bell and wave this ledger until I have your rent. And if you don't like it, you can just step outside and I'll punch you so hard you won't remember to say ouch. Come on out here, you miserable lowlife deadbeat!"

Other forms: Belligerence *(noun)*; belligerently *(adv)*

Note: The root "belli" has to do with fighting or war. Connect this word with "bellicose," which has almost the same meaning.

Sentence: The angry customer's *belligerence* made it hard for the saleswoman to remain polite.

BENEDICTION (ben-neh-DIK-shun) *noun* — **good wishes; a blessing**

Sounds like: Benedict shine

Picture: Benedict, who always says good and encouraging things to people, so that they come away from him shining with happiness. Note: Any word beginning with the prefix "bene-" has a positive meaning, and usually refers to a good result (or <u>bene</u>fit).

Sentence: The minister delivered a *benediction* before the ceremony.

BENEVOLENT (beh-NEV-oh-lent) *adj* — **kindhearted; good-natured; generous**

Sounds like: Ben Elephant

Picture: A kindly old elephant named Ben who lives at the zoo. He saves the peanuts that visitors give him and takes them to the other animals late at night. "That Ben Elephant," says one bear to another, "what a nice guy!"

Other forms: Benevolence *(noun);* benevolently *(adv)*

Sentence: Miserable and greedy for most of his life, the man became *benevolent* during his last years.

BENIGN (beh-NINE) *adj* — **gentle; kind-hearted; mild**

Sounds like: be nine

Picture: A machine that measures a person's kindness level. Its meter ranges from 1 to 9, with 9 designated as "extremely kind and gentle." A girl places the electrode helmet on her head, pulls the lever, and prays, "Oh, I hope I'm a nine! Be nine! Please be nine!"

Other form: Benignly *(adv)*

Sentence: Albert had a reputation for being a bully, but deep down he was a *benign* soul.

BEQUEATH (be-KWEETH) *verb* — **to leave behind or hand down through a will; transmit**

Rhymes with: beneath

Picture: The reading of a will. "...And to my son, Robert, who always thought my possessions were beneath him, I bequeath something that *is* beneath him: the rug on the floor in this room."

Other forms: Bequeathal, bequest *(nouns)*

Sentence: Many people *bequeath* large sums of money to their favorite charities.

BLIGHT (BLITE) *noun* — **decay; disease; widespread death**

Looks like: B light

Picture: An entire orchard of fruit trees has died. A scientist hired to study the situation concludes: "The problem is too much B-light. B-light is that part of the light spectrum emitted by car headlights. These trees were too close to the road, and the headlights wiped them out."

Sentence: When a main crop is hit with *blight*, widespread famine may result.

BOLSTER (BOLE-ster) *verb* — **to support; to reinforce**

Sounds like: bowl stir

Picture: A mixing bowl, filled with cake batter, is talking to the wooden spoon: "Come on spoon, stir that batter. I know you can do it!" (The batter joins in: "Hey, you're really bolstering the spoon's confidence! This cake may just pan out after all!")

Sentence: Nancy's goal of a scholarship was *bolstered* by an unexpected A in Biology.

BOMBAST (BOMM-bast) *noun* — **speech or writing intended to impress the audience; pompous**

Sounds like: bomb blast

Picture: A convention of scientists who specialize in explosives. The speaker is talking about his latest discovery: "Ladies and gentlemen, without bragging I must tell you that this invention will change the world. My bomb fits in the palm of the hand, yet one such device produces a blast that can destroy all of North America and rattle teacups in London. It is, probably, the greatest single advance in the history of mankind, if I may say so..."

Other form: Bombastic *(adj)*

Sentence: The newcomer's *bombast* offended the town's more mild-mannered residents.

BREVITY (BREV-uh-tee) *noun* — **briefness; conciseness**

Sounds like: Bravo Tea

Picture: Tea that takes just a few seconds to make. Also, when people drink Bravo Tea, they say what they have to say in very few words. It gives them the gift of brevity.

Sentence: Employers are busy people, so *brevity* is important in a resume.

BUMPTIOUS (BUMP-shuss) *adj* — **pushy; obnoxiously self-assertive**

Sounds like: bump chess

Picture: A man and woman are playing chess. The man is annoying, pushy, and rude. Whenever he captures one of his opponent's pieces, he bumps it off the board and yells out, "Bump chess! I love this game! And I really love winning!"

Sentence: The *bumptious* car salesman scared customers away.

CACOPHONY (kuh-KAH-fuh-nee) *noun* — **harshness of sound; opposite of harmony**

Looks like: a combination of "cocoon" and "symphony"

Picture: A cocoon hanging from the branch of a tree. Inside, a caterpillar on his way to becoming a butterfly has decided to make good use of the time by learning to play the violin. On this particular day, the caterpillar is playing an entire symphony, although not very well. Outside, birds and squirrels are covering their ears, trying to escape the cacophony coming from the cocoon.

Other form: Cacophonous *(adj)*   Note: The root "phone" has to do with sound, as in "telephone."

Sentence: New visitors to the rainforest are struck by the *cacophony*.

CAJOLE (cuh-JOLE) *verb* — **to fool with flattery or false promises; coax; deceive**

Sounds like: cage hole

Picture: A large cat sits outside a parakeet's cage. The cage has a small hole at the top. Inside, a parakeet is perched on a swing. "You have the most beautiful feathers," says the cat. "The colors are magnificent. Why don't you squeeze out through that hole so I can get a better look at you?"

Other forms: Cajolery, cajolement *(nouns)*

Sentence: The con-artist *cajoled* them out of their money.

MISS DOOR, LET ME BE CANDID... YOUR KNEES ARE KNOBBY, YOU BECOME UNHINGED WHEN THE TEMPO CHANGES, AND YOU NEVER SEEM TO KNOW IF YOU'RE OPENING OR CLOSING. I'M NOT KNOCKING YOU, BUT DON'T RING OUR BELL, WE'LL RING YOURS.

CANDOR (CANNED-er) *noun* — **honesty; frankness**

Looks like: can door

Picture: A door on stage. The door is trying out for a dance job. The producer, a tin can, is delivering the bad news with as much honesty as possible.

Other forms: Candid *(adj)*; candidly *(adv)*

Sentence: Political *candor* is refreshing.

CAPACIOUS (cuh-PAY-shuss) *adj* — **large; roomy; spacious**

Sounds like: car patients

Picture: A doctor who uses a car as her office. She explains: "This car has an incredible amount of space inside. The front seat is a waiting area and the back seat has three separate examining rooms."

Other forms: Capaciousness *(noun)*

Sentence: He needed a *capacious* apartment for his stuffed moose collection.

CAPITULATE (kuh-PITCH-oo-late) *verb* — **surrender; yield**

Looks like: capital late

Picture: The government of a small nation has just been overthrown by a neighboring country. In the capital city of the overthrown nation, the president is speaking with his military commander, who has just arrived with troops. "I'm sorry," he says, "but you got here too late. I was forced to surrender."

Other form: Capitulation *(noun)*

Sentence: The police refused to *capitulate* to the demands of the kidnapper.

CAPRICIOUS (cuh-PREE-shuss) *adj* — **unpredictable**

Looks like: cap riches

Picture: A man standing in front of a slot machine in a casino. He puts a quarter into the slot, pulls the handle, and holds his cap under the chute, waiting hopefully for his riches. He doesn't know if or when it will happen, but he's sure it *could* happen.

Other forms: Capriciously *(adv)*; caprice *(noun)*

Sentence: It's hard to plan a vacation when the weather can be so *capricious*.

CASTIGATE (CASS-tig-ate) *verb* — **scold; punish**

Sounds like: curse the gate

Picture: Someone scolding a gate.

Synonyms: Admonish, berate, censure, chasten, chastise, denounce, disparage, objurgate, rebuke, reprimand, reprove, upbraid.

Sentence: The angry judge *castigated* the lawyer.

CAUSTIC (CAWSE-tik) *adj* — **burning, either with chemicals or sarcasm**

Sounds like: caw stick

Picture: A crow crying ("caw, caw") because it has been burned by a stick coated with acid.

Sentence: The teacher's *caustic* criticism embarrassed his student.

CELERITY (seh-LEHR-ih-tee) *noun* — **speed**

Looks like: celery

Picture: A stalk of celery moving at high speed. The celery might be in the form of a race car zooming around the track.

Connect with: Accelerate.

Sentence: Drivers stuck in traffic may dream of *celerity*.

CENSURE (SEN-shur) *verb* — **to criticize**

Sounds like: send ashore

Picture: A man wading to shore from a large sailing ship. He is the navigator of the ship, and has been sent ashore by the captain and the rest of the crew because they blame him for getting them lost at sea. They have sent him to ask directions. As he walks, they shout at him from the ship: "You couldn't find your way across a bathtub!" "Try not to miss the beach!"

Note: Don't confuse with "censor," which means "to delete objectionable material."

Sentence: The newspaper editorial *censured* the governor for her budget proposals.

CHASTEN (CHAY-sen) *verb* — **punish; discipline; castigate**

Sounds like: chase sin

Picture: An old-fashioned, religious mother who is trying to discipline her mischievous son: "I'll keep scolding and punishing until I've chased the sin right out of you!"

Connect with: Chastise. Don't confuse with "chaste," which means "pure."

22   Sentence: Harshly *chastened* by his owner, the dog hid under the porch for three days.

CHASTISE (CHASS-tize) *verb* — **scold; punish; castigate**

Sounds like: chase ties

Picture: The same man who yelled at the gate (see CASTIGATE) is now chasing ties around the yard, scolding them.

Sentence: Roberta *chastised* her son for his low grades.

CHOLER (KAH-ler) *noun* — **anger**

Sounds like: collar

Picture: A dog who's angry about the ridiculous collar he has to wear.

Other form: Choleric *(adj)*

Sentence: Frustration and *choler* swept through the prison population.

CIRCUMSCRIBE (SIR-kum-skribe) *verb* — **draw a line around; define limits; confine; restrict**

Looks like: circus crib

Picture: The baby elephant is headed for a career in the circus, but she has a lot to learn. Her trainer puts the elephant in a baby crib and places the crib inside one of the circus rings. The elephant may climb out of the crib, but may not go outside the circle. Her movements have been circumscribed.

Other forms: Circumscribable *(adj)*; circumscription *(noun)*

Note: The prefix "circum" means "around." Think about the following words, and look up the ones you don't know: circumcise, circumference, circumlocution, circumnavigate, circumspect, circumvent.

Sentence: The movements of a fish in an aquarium are *circumscribed* by the size of the tank.

CIRCUMSPECT (SIR-kum-spekt) *adj* — **cautious**

Sounds like: search inspect

Picture: The chipmunk peeks out from her home — a hole in the trunk of a hollow tree. She must go out for food, but before leaving the safety of her tree, she carefully and methodically looks around (searches and inspects) to see if a predator is waiting to snatch her.

Other form: Circumspection *(noun)*

Sentence: In some situations, it's wiser to be *circumspect* rather than bold.

CLEMENCY (KLEM-en-see) *noun* — **mercy**

Sounds like: clam in sea

Picture: A clam as judge presiding over an undersea courtroom. The defendant is a mussel accused of fixing races at the snail track. Judge: "The maximum sentence for this crime is one weekend on a dry beach filled with small children and biology teachers. But it's your first offense, so I'll show clemency. I hereby sentence you to eight hours of voluntary service working with oil spill survivors."

Other form: Clement *(adj)*

Sentence: The remorseful defendant begged the judge for *clemency*.

OK, PRIVACY CAN BE REALLY NICE, BUT PEARL, IT'S BEEN 9 YEARS!

KNOCK KNOCK

CLOISTER (CLOY-ster) *noun* — **secluded or isolated from the outside world; also, a place of seclusion**

Sounds like: closed oyster

Picture: A giant closed oyster. Someone is hiding inside the shell.

Sentence: During the trial, the jury remained *cloistered* in a motel.

COALESCE (KO-uh-less) *verb* — **unite; grow together**

Sounds like : coal S

Picture: A man puts some charcoal into his barbecue grill, throws in a match, and goes into the house. When he returns, he sees that the coals have come together to form a large letter "S" at the bottom of the grill. "Wow, when they say it makes a Super Fire, they aren't kidding!"

Other forms: Coalescent *(adj);* coalescence *(noun)*

Sentence: Astronomers believe stars *coalesce* from huge clouds of gas.

COERCE (ko-ERSE) *verb* — **to force someone by threatening or physically overpowering him**

Sounds like: course

Picture: A young Army private has to run an obstacle course, which requires him to climb a flaming wall, swim across a pond filled with alligators, and run through a field of rattle-snakes. He's reluctant to run the course, but his sergeant forces him with threats of physical harm, verbal abuse, isolation, double shifts in the mess hall, and courtmartial.

Other forms: Coercion *(noun);* coercive *(adj);* coercively *(adv)*

Sentence: Steve tried to *coerce* his younger brother into mowing the lawn.

COMPLACENT (kum-PLAY-sent) *adj* — **self-satisfied; unconcerned**

Sounds like: come play, cent

Picture: A penny sits on a park bench. Two small children call to him, "Come play, Cent!" But the penny, smiling, hands behind head, eyes closed, is too self-satisfied to move from the bench.

Other forms: Complacence, complacency *(nouns)*

Sentence: Facing a less-talented opponent, it's easy to grow *complacent* and blow a big game.

COMPLIANT (kum-PLY-ent) *adj* — **following someone else's demands; conforming; obeying**

Looks almost exactly like: complaint

Picture: The man working in the complaint department of a store has put up a sign over his desk that says, "COMPLAINT." His boss has walked by nine or ten times, and each time has told the man to change the spelling to "COMPLIANT." Even though he knows it's incorrect, the employee gives in and makes the change. So now he works directly under a sign that says, "COMPLIANT."

Other forms: Compliance *(noun);* comply *(verb)*

24   Sentence: Employers who are domineering usually try to hire *compliant* people.

COMPOSURE (kum-POE-zher) *noun* — **calmness; equanimity**

Sounds like: Camp Pozer

Picture: A summer camp, called Camp Pozer, where the counselors and campers lie down all day long. Everyone is always calm and relaxed. Awards are given out for the longest naps.

Other form: Compose *(verb)*

Sentence: The bride tried to maintain her *composure* as the wedding cake fell onto the dance floor.

CONCEDE (kun-SEED) *verb* — **admit reluctantly; yield**

Sounds like: corn seed

Picture: Two farmers. One, examining something under a magnifying glass, admits that it *is* corn seed.

Other form: Concession *(noun)* (A concession speech is one in which the loser of an election reluctantly admits that his or her opponent has won.)

Sentence: The boss had to *concede* that it was his assistant's idea.

I GUESS YOU'RE RIGHT... IT **IS** CORN SEED

CONCISE (kun-SISE) *adj* — **short and to the point; terse**

Sounds like: Kahn's Ice

Picture: A company, called "Kahn's Ice," that sells and delivers blocks of ice. The slogan on their truck is "Cold."

Other forms: Conciseness *(noun);* concisely *(adv)*

Sentence: Phil read the *concise* note from his wife: "Leave. Now."

CONCUR (kun-KERR) *verb* — **agree**

Sounds like: can curl

Picture: Two hairstylists discussing a customer's hair. "I believe it can curl," says one. The other concurs, or agrees.

Other form: Concurrence *(noun)*

Sentence: Scientists do not *concur* on what caused the dinosaurs to die out.

CONDONE (kun-DONE) *verb* — **to overlook, excuse, or pardon**

Looks like: condo one

Picture: The owner of a condominium complex is showing her brother around. At condo one, he notices that the tenants have covered the outside of the building with multi-colored aluminum siding, placed a huge neon sign that flashes "We're number 1!" in the living room window, and trimmed the shrubs to look like characters from *Gilligan's Island*. When he asks why she would condone these changes, she replies, "They pay their rent."

Note: Don't confuse with "condemn," which means "to criticize."

Sentence: It's hard to *condone* such rude behavior.

CONFOUND (kon-FOUND) *verb* — **to mix up (in your own mind); or, to confuse someone else**

Sounds like: gun found

Picture: A detective investigating a murder. The victim was found in a windowless room, the door locked from the inside. The murder weapon, a gun, is found inside a locked cabinet, along with the keys to both the door and the cabinet itself. "I'm confounded," admits the bewildered detective.

Sentence: Magicians *confound* their audiences with a lot of distracting movement.

CONSONANCE (KON-so-nence) *noun* — **a blending of sounds or opinions; harmony; agreement**

Sounds exactly like: consonants

Picture: Three consonants from the alphabet — C, K, and Q — are having lunch together. "As far as I'm concerned," says C, "we're in complete agreement. We're all making the same sounds."

Other form: Consonant *(adj)*

Sentence: A committee starts out with many differing ideas, but tries to work toward *consonance*.

CONSUMMATE (KON-soo-mate) *verb* — **to complete or make whole**

Looks like: consume mate

Picture: Black widow spiders have a bizarre end to their mating ritual. After mating is complete, the female actually consumes (eats) the male. Imagine that the male and female come to this agreement beforehand. They shake (consummating the deal), then after consummating the mating ritual, the female consumes her mate (consummating this really disgusting law of nature).

Other forms: Consummation *(noun);* consummate *(adj)*   Note: As an adjective, "consummate" (KON-soo-met) means "perfect" or "highly-skilled."

Sentence: They *consummated* the successful meeting with a lavish banquet.

CONTEND (kun-TEND) *verb* — **to argue a point or position; or, to struggle for**

Sounds like: can't end

Picture: A football team, losing 118 to 0. In the locker room at halftime, the captain speaks up: "We've fought back all year and it <u>can't end</u> here. If we're to be <u>contenders</u>, we can't give up!"

Other forms: Contention *(noun);* contentious *(adj)*

Sentence: The driver tried to *contend* that the stop sign was hidden by the tree.

CONTINGENT (kun-TIN-jent) *adj* — **dependent upon other circumstances; conditional**

Sounds like: can tin gent

Picture: A man made of tin cans. A friend asks if he's planning to play in the golf tournament next weekend. "It depends," says the can tin gent. "If it's sunny, I'll be there. If it rains, I definitely won't. I haven't played in ten years, so I'm rusty enough already."

Other form: Contingency *(noun);* contingently *(adv)*

Sentence: His release from jail was *contingent* upon his promise to show up in court.

26

CONTRACT (kun-TRAKT) *verb* — **squeeze together; shrink**

Looks exactly like: contract (KON-trakt) — a legal document

Picture: Two businesspeople are making a deal of some kind. After they each sign the contract, the document begins to shrink, as if the paper it's written on is being compressed. Says one of the signers, "I thought this deal would allow me to expand, but it appears as though it will be just the opposite."

Other forms: Contraction *(noun);* contractible *(adj)*

Sentence: Most matter *contracts* when it freezes; however, water expands.

CONTRITE (kun-TRITE) *adj* — **sorry; penitent**

Sounds like: canned trout

Picture: A large, overfed cat has been discovered in the pantry after he's opened and devoured twelve cans of trout. As his owner hovers angrily over him, the cat appears to be sorry; his face and body seem to be saying, "I promise, I'll never do this again." (The dog of the house watches from a corner of the room and thinks, "I wonder if the cat would teach me how to use that can opener.")

Other form: Contrition *(noun)*

Sentence: Genuinely *contrite*, Debbie confessed to eating all the doughnuts.

CONUNDRUM (kah-NUN-drum) *noun* — **riddle; mystery**

Looks like: cone and drum

Picture: A man playing the drum, but instead of drumsticks, he's using ice cream cones. An observer asks: "How does he play music with those things?" A second observer: "It's a mystery to me."

Sentence: The more scientists learn about the universe, the more of a *conundrum* it appears to be.

CONVERGE (kun-VERJ) *verb* — **move together to meet at a common point**

Sounds like: can merge

Picture: Two separate highways have been re-routed so that the cars *can merge* into one flow of traffic. These roads now converge.

Other forms: Convergence *(noun);* convergent *(adj)*

Sentence: Parallel lines never *converge*.

CONVICTION (kun-VIK-shun) *noun* — **an opinion that is strongly held**

Sounds like: convict Shawn

Picture: You're part of a jury working on the trial of a man named Shawn. The prosecutor is addressing his opening remarks to the jury: "I believe with all my heart that Shawn is guilty. I *know* he committed this terrible crime. When you see the evidence, you'll also be sure. And you will convict Shawn."

Sentence: Betty held to her *convictions*, despite the pressure from her colleagues.

CONVIVIAL (kun-VIV-ee-yul) *adj* — **fond of parties; sociable**

Looks like: can Vivian
Sounds (a little) like: carnival

Picture: The director from CANDOR. His sister Vivian (also a can) has just opened her own carnival. Can Vivian is the perfect host, because she's so festive and outgoing. She greets every guest at the front gate and introduces them to other visitors.

Other forms: Conviviality *(noun);* convivially *(adv)*

Sentence: It can be stressful when one member of a couple is *convivial* and the other is a loner.

COPIOUS (KO-pee-us) *adj* — **in large quantity; abundant**

Sounds like: copy us

Picture: A classroom with three teachers at the blackboard. Each is filling his or her board with notes. One says to the students, "Copy us. You'll have copious notes by the end of this course!"

Other form: Copiousness *(noun)*

Connect with: Cornu<u>copia</u>

Sentence: It was a lavish party with *copious* food and drink.

CORDIAL (KOR-jil) *adj* — **friendly; welcoming; gracious**

Sounds like: cord Jill

Picture: A girl named Jill who stands at the post office and hands out cord to customers in case they need to tie up packages. She is known to everyone as the warmest, friendliest person in town.

Other forms: Cordiality *(noun);* cordially *(adv)*

Sentence: We'd heard she was a grouch, so we were surprised by her *cordial* welcome.

CORPOREAL (kor-POR-ee-ul) *adj* — **having to do with the body or the physical world**

Looks like: corporal

Picture: An Army corporal has become known on the base for his addiction to physical fitness. He is constantly doing push-ups and sit-ups, jogging, or lifting weights. When asked why he spends so much time exercising, the corporal explains that "the body is the most important part of a person and it must be kept in perfect condition." When the corporal is invited by friends to attend a religious ceremony, he responds, "Sorry, but I have no interest in the spirit or the soul or any of those religious ideas. Just the body. I'm going to lift weights all day today."

Other forms: Corporealness *(noun);* corporeally *(adv)*

Connect with: Corporation (a body of people), corpse (a dead body), and corpulent (having a large, overweight body)

Sentence: If there are ghosts, how do they interact with the *corporeal* world?

CORROBORATE (ker-OBB-er-ate) *verb* — **support with evidence; tell the same story; confirm**

Sounds like: co-robber eight

Picture: Eight people have been arrested and brought to trial for the same robbery. One by one, each of the eight "co-robbers" testifies on the witness stand, carefully answering the prosecutor's questions in exactly the same way the previous person did. So each corroborates the testimony of the others.

Other forms: Corroboration *(noun)*; corroborative *(adj)*   Note: Usually used to describe courtroom testimony or evidence. Don't confuse with "collaborate."

Sentence: Scientists continue to find evidence that *corroborates* Einstein's theories.

CRITERIA (cry-TEER-ee-uh) *noun* — **requirements or standards used to make a decision**

Sounds like: cry tearier

Picture: The director is advising an actress who is trying out for a role in the show: "When you get to the part where you find out your horse has died, you must cry tearier. We're using this scene to make our decision about who gets the part, and the more tears, the better your chances."

Other form: Criterion *(singular)*

Sentence: There must be many *criteria* for selecting astronauts who will travel to Mars.

CRYPTIC (KRIP-tik) *adj* — **hidden; secret; mysterious**

Sounds like: crypt tack

Think of: *Crypt* means tomb or underground vault. Imagine someone looking around above ground for a tack, but she can't find it because it's buried in the crypt. She holds a piece of paper that says: "Don't bother looking for the tack — it's below you." "Hmmm," she thinks, "that's a pretty cryptic message."

Sentence: The directions on the map are *cryptic*, which may be why nobody has found the treasure.

CULPABLE
(CULP-uh-bull) *adj* — **guilty; blameworthy**

Sounds like: gulpable

Picture: A boy has done something wrong and is being questioned by his mother. He swallows hard, making a "gulp" sound.

Other form: Culpability *(noun)* Connect with: Culprit

Sentence: Found to be *culpable*, he was fined.

CUPIDITY (cue-PID-ih-tee) *noun* — **greed, especially for money**

Looks like: cupid

Picture: Cupid using his bow and arrow to hold up a bank.

Sentence: The burglar returned to the house for more, and his *cupidity* is what got him caught.

29

CURSORY (KERR-sir-ee) *adj* — **quickly and incompletely done; superficial**

Looks like: curse sorry

Picture: A witch who'd changed a woman's husband into a cocker spaniel. Touched by the wife's woeful pleas, the witch admits feeling bad about inflicting the curse, and agrees to change the husband back into a man. But in her haste she doesn't complete the job: he's still half dog.

Sentence: Pressed for time, the captain conducted a *cursory* inspection.

DAUNTED (DAWN-ted) *adj* — **dismayed; disheartened; discouraged (made less courageous)**

Sounds like: dawn Ted

Picture: Ted is trying to cross the desert. When he awakens at dawn and looks around, he realizes he'd been walking in circles all night. Now he's about to give up his effort. "I was undaunted," Ted says to himself, "and then came the dawn."

Other forms: Daunt *(verb)*; dauntless, daunting *(adj)*; dauntlessly *(adv)*

Sentence: Reaching the South Pole was a *daunting* challenge for many explorers.

DECADENCE (DEK-uh-dents) *noun* — **moral decay or decline**

Sounds like: deck of dance

Picture: Two very conservative ladies aboard a cruise ship. They're discussing what goes on down on the dance deck. "It's disgusting," says one. "They get drunk and they dance all night..." "They're animals," says the other. "That's all I can say. They're morally-corrupt, filthy, and decadent."

Other forms: Decadent *(adj)*; decadently *(adv)*

NOTE: Don't be fooled by the fact that many restaurants like to describe their desserts as "decadent." This word does NOT mean delicious, wonderful, or anything positive.

Sentence: Some historians attribute the fall of the Roman Empire to internal *decadence*.

DEFAME (de-FAME) *verb* — **to say things harmful to a person's reputation; malign; vilify**

Sounds like: the frame

Think of: A very valuable picture frame that had been stored at a fine art museum. When the frame disappears, the guilty museum curator tells everyone the cleaning lady stole it, and that she's been stealing from the museum for years. He is defaming her.

Other forms: Defamation *(noun)*; defamatory *(adj)*

Sentence: The man was *defamed* by the accusations of criminal conduct.

DEFERENCE (DEFF-er-ense) *noun* — **the act of yielding to someone else out of respect**

Sounds like: deafer ants

Picture: A family of ants arriving at a music hall. All the ants in this family have trouble with their hearing, but the grandparents are nearly deaf. The younger members of the family, acknowledging that the grandparents are deafer, allow them to sit in the front, closest to the musicians.

Other forms: Defer *(verb)*; deferential *(adj)*

Sentence: In *deference* to his boss, Milton refused to take credit for the discovery.

DENOUNCE (dee-NOWNCE) *verb* — **criticize; condemn**

Sounds like: dean ounce

Picture: A short, thin college dean, named Dean Ounce, who criticizes everything and everyone at his school. He yells at students: "You're all lazy and dumb and a disgrace to this institution." One of the students says to another, "Pound-for-pound, Dean Ounce is the most critical dean we've ever had."

Other form: Denunciation *(noun)*

Sentence: The president *denounced* the actions of his country's closest ally.

DEPLETED (dee-PLEET-id) *verb* — **emptied; drained; used up**

Sounds like: the pleated

Picture: Saleswoman to a customer who is looking through a rack of pants. "I'm sorry," she says, "the pleated ones are all gone."

Other form: Depletion *(noun);* depletable *(adj)*

Sentence: The epidemic became a medical emergency when supplies of the antibiotic were *depleted*.

DEPLORE (dee-PLOR) *verb* — **to express regret or disapproval; complain; criticize**

Sounds like: deep lure

Picture: Two fish in the ocean, discussing a fisherman's baited hook. First fish: "Pathetic. We're five hundred feet down and we have to look at plastic worms? Why would anyone use such deep lures, anyway?" Second fish: "I guess they're just not interested in those shallow fish that live upstairs."

Other form: Deplorable *(adj)*

Sentence: Visitors *deplored* the terrible conditions in which local residents were living.

DEPRECATE (DEPP-rah-kate) *verb* — **disapprove; belittle**

Sounds like: Debra Kate

Picture: Debra Kate, Dean Ounce's sister (see DENOUNCE). Debra Kate is the headmistress at a girls' boarding school. She is very strict and old-fashioned. Like her brother, she believes her role is to express disapproval, and she always lets her students know how unhappy she is with them.

Other form: Deprecatory *(adj)*

Note: Don't confuse with "depreciate," which has to do with lowering the value of something.

Sentence: People liked his self-*deprecating* sense of humor.

DERIDE (dee-RIDE) *verb* — **make fun of; ridicule**

Sounds like: the ride

Picture: An amusement park. Two men are laughing uncontrollably at their friend who has just gotten off "The Ride," a roller coaster that obviously frightened the man a great deal. One of them says, "Maybe you'd better stick with the kiddie rides!"

Other form: Derision *(noun)*

Sentence: Lester was *derided* every day at work for his unusual taste in clothes.

DESPONDENT (dih-SPON-dent) *adj*
— **feeling hopeless or depressed**

Sounds like: the spoon dent

Picture: A man with a very large collection of antique spoons. He sits holding a dented spoon in one hand, his face buried in the other as he cries to his wife.

Other form: Despondency *(noun)*

Sentence: After the fire, Sam was *despondent* for days.

DESTITUTE (DESS-tih-toot) *adj*
— **poor; lacking possessions**

Sounds like: dusty tooth

Picture: A man so poor that he has only one tooth left (he can't afford dental care). And even that one tooth is dusty, because he doesn't own a toothbrush.

Other form: Destitution *(noun)*

Sentence: In order to qualify for the scholarship, you had to be almost *destitute*.

DEXTERITY (dex-TERR-ih-tee) *noun* — **high level of skill, especially with the hands; adroitness**

Sounds like: Decks Terry

Picture: A magician named Terry who is so skillful with cards that he's known as "Decks Terry." (Some say he can shuffle a deck of cards while they're still in the box.)

Other form: Dexterous *(adj)*
Connect with: Ambidextrous

Sentence: My grandmother's *dexterity* helped her produce beautiful quilts.

32

DESPOT (DESS-pot) *noun* — **tyrant**

Looks like: desk pot

Picture: A pot standing on a desk, proclaiming to be in complete power.

Other forms: Despotism *(noun)*; despotic *(adj)*

Sentence: After assuming control, he turned into a *despot*.

DESULTORY (DESS-ul-tor-ee) *adj* — **lacking a plan; aimless**

Sounds like: this dull story

Picture: The father of the groom has gone up to the microphone to toast the newlyweds. As he begins to speak, the groom says, "Oh no, not *this dull story*! He just rambles on and on. He doesn't even think about what he wants to say until he gets up there!" (The father begins: "Ladies and gentlemen. Friends and family. Guests. Waiters and waitresses. Thank you for sharing this special day with us. You know, when my son was eleven, some things happened. I don't necessarily know what they are, or even think they have much to do with this very special day. And now that he has taken a bride, I often wonder...")

Other form: Desultoriness *(noun)*

Sentence: The team leader's *desultory* approach to the project frustrated everyone.

DIATRIBE (DIE-a-tribe) *noun* — **a bitterly critical speech**

Sounds like: dye a tribe

Picture: The chief is enraged, screaming at a man who has dyed the entire tribe green.

Sentence: When something went wrong, he went into a *diatribe*.

DIGRESS (dye-GRESS) *verb* — **to move away from the main topic when writing or speaking; to go off on a tangent**

Sounds like: die grass

Picture: The guest speaker at the American Lawn Club's annual convention. The speaker's topic is "How to Bring Dead Grass Back to Life." Just a few minutes into his talk, while discussing the problem of dead grass under the barbecue grill, the lecturer begins to tell his audience about a really fun cookout he went to when he was visiting his sister in Arkansas, and the great recipe she gave him for shish kebab, and how his brother-in-law, Mark, cheated at Monopoly, and...

Other form: Digression *(noun)*   Sentence: In writing, if you *digress* from the main point for too long, you may lose your reader.

DILATORY (DILL-uh-torr-ee) *adj* — **causing lateness; stalling**

Looks like: delay story

Picture: A little girl who doesn't want to go to the dentist. She starts to tell her mother a long story about her day at school. Her mother says, "This is just a 'delay story' because you want us to be late."

Sentence: His *dilatory* actions caused them to miss their plane.

DISCERNING (dih-SURR-ning) *adj* — **insightful; perceptive**

Sounds like: this urn Ning

Picture: Two archeologists digging at a site in China. They uncover a vase, or urn, and one of the archeologists begins to describe it after a very brief examination: "This urn? Ning. That is, it's from the Ning Dynasty. It's easy to tell. See this pattern of dragon's teeth along the bottom? That's distinctive of Ning. Also, the color and shape of the handles are clues that this urn is from the Ning Dynasty." The second archeologist adds, "Also, it says right here on the bottom, 'Made during the Ning Dynasty.'"

Other forms: Discern *(verb);* discernible *(adj)*   Sentence: She has a *discerning* nature, which allows her to understand her clients on a deep level.

DISCLOSE (diss-KLOZE) *verb* — **provide information; reveal**

Sounds like: this close

Picture: Two corporate chairmen are in a meeting. A vice president of one of the companies comes out of the meeting to talk secretly with waiting reporters. Holding two fingers a quarter-inch apart, he whispers, "They're this close to making the deal." Then he says, "But you didn't hear that from *me*."

Other form: Disclosure *(noun)* Sentence: Sue *disclosed* more to the stranger than she'd intended.   33

DISCORD (DISS-kord) *noun* — **disagreement; dissonance**

Sounds like: this chord

Picture: Four people listening to music and trying to decide what a certain chord is. They all have different opinions. "This chord is C," says one. "No, it isn't," says another, "this chord is F..."

Other forms: Discordant *(adj);* discordantly *(adv)*

Sentence: A certain amount of *discord* is expected within every family.

DISCOURSE (DISS-korse) *noun* — **exchange of ideas; conversation**

Sounds like: this course

Picture: A college professor, on the first day of class, explaining what the course will be about. "This course is called, 'On the Nature of Talk.' We will explore the history of conversation. We will study videotapes of people talking. We will discuss the art of discussion. All tests will be oral. And I will insist on plenty of talking in class, because *this course* is about *discourse*."

Sentence: We anticipated a heated debate, but the *discourse* remained civil.

DISDAIN (diss-DANE) *noun* — **a feeling of scorn or contempt**

Sounds like: this stain

Picture: Person who refuses to help others remove a stain (he's above that sort of work).

CLEAN UP A STAIN? THAT'S BELOW ME.

Other forms: Disdain *(verb);* disdainful *(adj)*

Sentence: Ethel loved her son, but treated his wife with *disdain*.

DISPARAGE (dis-PAHR-ij) *verb* — **say negative things; belittle**

Sounds like: this asparagus

Picture: Two vegetable farmers stand along a fence looking over to the other side, where a third farmer is loading his asparagus crop onto a truck. They are ridiculing him for the small asparagus he's grown. "Asparagus?" asks one. "I thought it was string beans!"

Other forms: Disparaging *(adj);* disparagingly *(adv)*   Note: Don't confuse with "disparate."

Sentence: No one likes to hear *disparaging* remarks (at least about themselves).

DISPARATE (dis-PAHR-et) *adj* — **different**

Sounds like: this parrot

Picture: A pet shop owner explaining to a customer, "This parrot is different from this parrot."

Other forms: Disparity *(noun);* disparately *(adv)*

Sentence: Most cities contain *disparate* ethnic groups.

34

DISPERSE (dis-PERSE) *verb* — **spread around; scatter**

Sounds like: this purse

Picture: A woman taking candy from her purse and throwing it to eagerly awaiting children.

Other form: Dispersion *(noun)*

Note: Don't confuse with "disburse," which means "to pay out."

Sentence: The police used tear gas to *disperse* the crowd.

DISSOLUTION (dis-so-LOOSH-un) *noun* — **separation into parts; the process of dissolving**

Sounds like: this solution

Picture: A chemist comes into the lab with a beaker of liquid. "This solution," she says, "must be separated into two parts." Then she pours half into one flask and half into another.

Other form: Dissolve *(verb)*

Sentence: Another way of saying divorce is "*dissolution* of marriage."

DISTENDED (dis-TEND-ed) *adj* — **swollen; extended**

Sounds like: this tendon (a tendon connects muscle to bone)

Picture: A man and woman are playing tennis. The match is several hours old when the man approaches the net with a sad face and an elbow swollen to seven times its normal size. "Sorry, but I have to stop. It's this tendon. It swells up every time I play."

Other forms: Distend *(verb)*; distension *(noun)*

Sentence: The toxins had greatly *distended* the man's body.

DISSENT (dis-SENT) *verb* — **to disagree, especially with the majority, or with an authority**

Sounds like: this scent

Picture: A crowd gathered in the capital of an unknown country. The king has just announced a "national scent" to go along with the national flag and national flower. The scent is lemon, and government workers have begun spraying the entire country with furniture polish. Many in the crowd disagree with the decision, holding up signs that say, "This scent is a lemon."

Other forms: Dissent, dissension *(nouns)*

Sentence: Totalitarian forms of government do not tolerate much *dissent* among their citizens.

DIVERGENCE (dye-VERR-jence) *noun* — **the act of splitting off into different directions**

Sounds like: diver gents

Picture: Two gentlemen diving from the same diving board, but in different directions. (Onlooker: "We're likely to get diverging accounts of this dive from the judges.")

Other forms: Diverge *(verb)*; divergent *(adj)*

Sentence: A *divergence* of opinion ended their friendship.

35

DIVERSE (dye-VERSE) *adj* — **different; various**

Sounds like: dye furs

Picture: The father rabbit has dyed his seven children different colors. He explains to his wife: "I dyed their fur so they all look different. Now we can tell them apart."

Other form: Diversity *(noun)*

Sentence: Many colleges are looking for well-rounded applicants with *diverse* experiences.

DOGMATIC (dawg-MAT-ik) *adj* — **sticking to long-held beliefs, even when faced with contrary evidence; closed-minded**

Sounds like: dog medic

Picture: A medic (military doctor) arguing with a dog. The medic is insisting that there is no scientific proof that dogs can talk. The dog replies, "I think you're ignoring some important evidence."

Other forms: Dogma, dogmatism *(nouns)*

Sentence: Religious *dogma* must somehow allow for social change.

ECLECTIC (ee-KLEK-tik) *adj* — **choosing from many different sources; carefully selective**

Looks like: electric

Picture: Two women talking in the kitchen. The visitor notices bills from six different electric companies for the same month. She asks about it. Her friend explains: "I like the electric heat I get from Eastwest Utilities, but I think the electricity from Superior Power is better for cooking. The lights are a little brighter since I started using Con Everyone Electric & Gas. And it just seems that the refrigerator keeps things colder with Central Illuminating. And then there's the hair dryer, and the VCR..."

Other form: Eclecticism *(noun)*

Sentence: An *eclectic* reader enjoys many different writing styles and subjects.

DOLEFUL (DOLE-full) *adj* — **extremely sad**

Sounds like: doll full

Think of: Doll full of tears. Picture a doll that cries and has a very sad expression.

Connect with: Dolorous, doldrums, and condolences

Sentence: Her *doleful* eyes told the story of a difficult life.

ECCENTRIC (ek-SEN-trik) *adj* — **different from most, especially in personality or behavior**

Sounds like: accent Rick

Picture: An old man named Rick who sits in a rocking chair on the sidewalk in front of his house and speaks in a different accent every five minutes. (The neighbors think he's a little weird.)

Other form: Eccentricity *(noun)*   Sentence: Alice was *eccentric*, but everyone loved her odd ways.

EFFACE (ee-FACE) *verb* — erase

Sounds like: the face, and rhymes with erase

Picture: A penny that has been worn from use, so that Lincoln's face has been erased.

Note: Don't confuse with *deface*, which means to mar or disfigure.

Sentence: All signs of poverty and suffering were *effaced* before the queen's visit.

EFFERVESCENCE (eff-er-VEH-sense) *noun* — **the quality of being bubbly or full of life**

Sounds like: ever pheasants

Picture: A large field surrounded by trees. The field is crowded with pheasants who are running around singing, dancing, and blowing enormous bubbles with those gigantic plastic rings and pans of soap suds. Two beavers look on, one saying to the other, "Ah, pheasants, ever pheasants. So bubbly. So full of life... Well, let's get back to work."

Other form: Effervescent *(adj)*

Sentence: She'd had little acting experience, but her *effervescence* got her the part.

EFFICACY (EF-ih-kuh-see) *noun* — **the ability to produce desired results**

Sounds like: Effie can see

Picture: A little girl named Effie has been legally blind since birth. But today her eye doctor has presented her with a special pair of glasses, and when she puts them on she can see quite well. "I believe you'll be happy," says the doctor, "with the efficacy of these eyeglasses."

Other forms: Efficacious *(adj)*; efficaciously *(adv)*

Sentence: The new medication had a higher degree of *efficacy*.

ELATED (ee-LAY-ted) *adj* — **extremely happy; overjoyed**

Sounds like: eel ate Ted

Picture: Mother eel to father eel: "Dear, I'm so happy! Baby eel ate Ted this morning! It's the first time he's eaten in weeks!" Father eel: "That's great, honey, but Ted was my brother. So now you're elated and I'm lugubrious." (Eels talk like that.)

Other form: Elation *(noun)*

Sentence: Uncle Frank was *elated* about winning the lottery.

ELOQUENCE (ELL-oh-kwence) *noun* — **powerfully effective speech**

Sounds like: elephants

Picture: The Republican National Convention. Thousands have gathered in the convention hall to hear the guest speaker, an elephant (the party's mascot). Everyone is dressed in elephant costumes. Elephant signs and posters are everywhere. "I'm all ears," says one audience member. "Many believe he's the best speaker in the country. And I'm told that once you hear him talk, you never forget it."

Other forms: Eloquent *(adj)*; eloquently *(adv)*

Sentence: Not usually known for *eloquence*, Ralph surprised everyone with a wonderful speech.

EMBELLISH (em-BEL-lish) *verb*
— **to make more beautiful; decorate; adorn**

Sounds like: M bell fish

Picture: A young girl showing her mother how she's decorated the fish in their goldfish bowl. The fish have bells hanging from their bodies, and each of the bells has the letter 'M' on it. "Look, Mommy," says the girl, "M Bell Fish!" "Oh, they're beautiful," says the mother, "and if they ever jump out of the bowl, we'll be able to hear them flopping around on the floor! Let's go decorate the hamsters!"

Other form: Embellishment *(noun)*

Sentence: Their home was plain and simple, but they *embellished* it with handmade crafts.

I RECOMMEND THE END HORSE.

ENDORSE (enn-DORSE) *verb*
— **promote; recommend**

Sounds like: end horse

Picture: A horse salesman saying to a customer, "I recommend the end horse."

Other form: Endorsement *(noun)*

Sentence: Celebrity *endorsements* can be effective.

EMULATE (EM-yoo-late) *verb* — **imitate**

Sounds like: Em, you're late

Picture: Emily is being scolded by her mother for getting home late: "Em, you're late." Standing right behind Emily is her younger brother, who says, "I'm late too, Mom, because I want to be just like Em."

Other form: Emulation *(noun)* Sentence: As young boys, we tried to *emulate* our favorite ballplayers.

ENDEMIC (en-DEMM-ik) *adj* — **native to a particular country or among a particular group**

Sounds like: end emic

Think of: A country where everyone gets a strange illness called Emic Disease. Symptoms include swollen eyebrows, wrinkled kneecaps, and a kind of a sneeze-cough-hiccup that keeps sufferers (and their families) awake for weeks at a time. One day, the entire population gathers to protest the government's apathy about the disease. Ten thousand people with swollen eyebrows and wrinkled kneecaps fill the capital city and, between sneeze-cough-hiccups, they chant, "End Emic."

Sentence: That particular plant is *endemic* to the northern tip of the island.

ENERVATE (ENN-er-vate) *verb* — **sap the strength; weaken**

Sounds like: enter wait

Picture: A man attempting to get onto an elevator. The elevator operator tells the man to enter, but every time he tries, the operator tells him to wait. After ten tries, the man is exhausted. "Enter, wait. Enter, wait." he says. "I'm drained. I think I'll take the stairs."

Other forms: Enervation *(noun);* enervative *(adj)*

Sentence: The hot sun *enervated* the runners, slowing their pace.

ENHANCE (enn-HANTS) *verb* — **intensify; improve**

Sounds like: in hands

Picture: A man and woman have locked themselves out of their car. As the man encourages her, the woman manages to insert a wire hanger through the key chain inside the car and pull the keys out through the slightly open window. With the keys in her hands she says, "Well, this should enhance our chances of getting home."

Other form: Enhancement *(noun)*

Sentence: A coat of paint can greatly *enhance* the appearance of a room.

ENIGMA (en-IGG-muh) *noun* — **mystery; puzzle**

Sounds like: an egg, Ma

Picture: A woman calling her mother from the maternity ward of a hospital, where she's just given birth to something unexpected: "This is hard to explain, but it's an egg, Ma." As she speaks, she glances over to the large egg in the crib next to her bed.

Other form: Enigmatic *(adj)*   Sentence: The origin of Saturn's rings remains a puzzling *enigma*.

ENMITY (ENN-mit-tee) *noun* — **mutual hatred**

Sounds like: enemy tee

Picture: Two people who completely hate each other are on the golf course together. They are about to tee off at the 'Enemy Tee,' where hostile players face each other with golf clubs and keep swinging until one of them has to be carried away. (Says one observer to another at the Enemy Tee, "This gives a whole new meaning to the term 'Grand Slam' event.")

Connect with: Amity *(noun)* — friendship. It's easy to tell these two words apart, because 'enmity' looks like 'enemy.'

Sentence: The *enmity* between the two warring nations is centuries old.

EPHEMERAL (ee-FEM-er-al) *adj* — **temporary; short-lived**

Sounds like: F. M. mural

Picture: An artist, known by just his initials ("F.M."), who paints murals that fade away very soon after he completes them.

Other form: Ephemerally *(adv)*

Sentence: My memory of dreams is *ephemeral*: by lunchtime, I can't remember a thing.

ERADICATE (er-AD-ih-kate) *verb* — **remove completely and permanently; exterminate**

Sounds like: a rat, a crate

Picture: Your house is infested with rats and you would prefer that it weren't, so you call an exterminator. He comes over the next day with a bunch of crates. You watch with some curiosity as he spreads the crates all over the house. You look for traps, poison, spray guns, but you see none of that stuff. Just crates. So you ask him what's up. "The rats love these crates," he explains. "You put a crate out, a rat will go inside and close the lid. Nobody knows this, actually, I discovered it. But it's true. The thing is, each rat wants its own crate. If you have a rat, I bring in a crate. A rat, a crate. Fifty rats, fifty crates. I come back tomorrow and take them all away forever and you'll never even know they were here."

Other forms: Eradication *(noun)*; eradicable *(adj)*

Sentence: Lisa worked hard to *eradicate* all evidence that her ex-husband had ever lived with her.

ERRATIC (er-RAT-ik) *adj* — **unpredictable; differing from what is normal or expected**

Sounds like: ear attic

Picture: A house. The owner has installed giant ears on either side of the house, up near the attic. The neighbors across the street are looking at the ears and discussing the owner of the house. One neighbor: "He's always been kind of unpredictable, but this is strange, even for him."

Other form: Erratically *(adv)* Note: Don't confuse with *erotic*.

Sentence: The sleepy man was driving *erratically*.

ERUDITION (err-yoo-DISH-un) *noun* — **the knowledge acquired through many years of study**

Sounds like: every edition

Picture: A student visiting his professor's office, where the walls are lined with many books. "Professor," asks the student, "have you read all these books?" The teacher responds: "Every edition."

Other forms: Erudite *(adj)*; eruditely *(adv)*

Sentence: The professor's *erudite* manner impressed many students, and intimidated others.

ESOTERIC (ess-oh-TERR-ik) *adj* — **known to, or understood by, a limited group of people**

Sounds like: it's so Derek

Picture: A group of men and boys attending a convention for people named Derek. Everyone at the Derek Convention is wearing a name tag that says, "Hello, My Name Is Derek," and they're all standing around talking about famous Dereks in history, telling Derek jokes, and thinking about the things that Dereks think about. An onlooker (named Jeffrey) says to a friend, "Don't ask *me* what they're talking about. I haven't understood one word they've said since I got here. It's all so, I don't know... it's so Derek."

Other form: Esoterica *(noun)*

Sentence: The book was filled with *esoteric* information about a long-lost tribe.

ETHEREAL (ee-THEER-ee-ul) *adj* — **heavenly; fine; delicately beautiful**

Sounds like: eat cereal

Picture: A beautiful angel with platinum hair, delicately smooth skin, and a glowing face comes down from the sky to tell everyone how to achieve such a heavenly state: "Eat cereal."

Other forms: Etherealness *(noun);* ethereally *(adv)*

Sentence: The frozen mist on the trees provided an *ethereal* backdrop for the photograph.

EULOGIZE (YOO-luh-jize) *verb* — **to praise highly; to extol**

Sounds like: your large eyes

Remember: In our culture, a eulogy is most often a speech given at a person's funeral. So picture the brother of the person who has died, speaking to his sister at her funeral (he's really speaking to the congregation, telling them about her). "You were the best sister anyone could hope for. You were sensitive, and understanding, and always willing to go out of your way to help someone in need. But what I'll always remember about you is *your large eyes*, filled with love and laughter."

Note: The prefix "eu-" almost always means "good." Look up eugenics, euphony, and euphoria in the dictionary, and see EUPHEMISM below.

Sentence: Listening to a *eulogy* helps us remember specific traits about the person who has died.

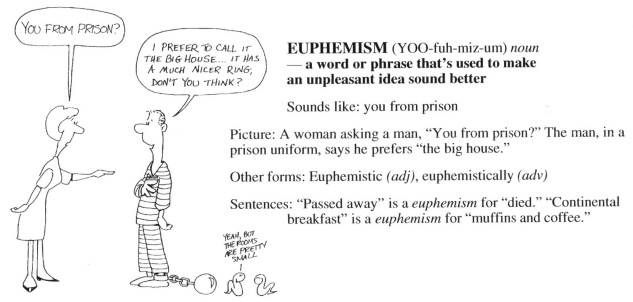

EUPHEMISM (YOO-fuh-miz-um) *noun* — **a word or phrase that's used to make an unpleasant idea sound better**

Sounds like: you from prison

Picture: A woman asking a man, "You from prison?" The man, in a prison uniform, says he prefers "the big house."

Other forms: Euphemistic *(adj)*, euphemistically *(adv)*

Sentences: "Passed away" is a *euphemism* for "died." "Continental breakfast" is a *euphemism* for "muffins and coffee."

EVASIVE (ee-VAY-siv) *adj* — **tending to avoid giving direct answers**

Looks like: Eva's hive

Picture: A bumble bee has flown his date, Eva, home. She lives in a condominium of hives, but doesn't want him to know which one. "So," he says, "which hive do you live in, Eva?" "Oh, one of those over there," she answers evasively. "Well, I better get some rest. Give me a buzz some time."

Other forms: Evade *(verb);* evasiveness *(noun)*

Sentence: The nervous witness avoided eye contact and his answers were *evasive*.

The following words begin with "ex". "Ex" sounds like "eggs," so in order to remember many of these words, we will create characters, situations, and stories involving eggs.

EXACERBATE (ex-ASS-er-bate) *verb* — to make a bad situation worse

Sounds like: eggs as her bait

Picture: A woman is fishing from a rowboat, using hard-boiled eggs as bait. Nearby, in another boat, is her doctor. He's worried about her cholesterol level, which is already too high. "She's eating fish. And to make matters worse, she's using eggs as her bait. She's going to exacerbate her condition."

Other form: Exacerbation *(noun)*

Sentence: Trying to put out a fire with gasoline will only *exacerbate* the problem.

EXPURGATE (EX-per-gate) *verb* — to remove offensive words, ideas, or symbols; censor

Sounds like: eggs pure gate

Picture: Someone has painted obscene graffiti on a gate. The eggs who live next-door are horrified, and immediately repaint the gate to return it to its pure condition.

Other form: Expurgatory *(adj)*

Sentence: Some people want to *expurgate* racist and sexist language from literature.

EXALT (egg-ZAWLT) *verb* — raise in rank; elevate; praise

Sounds like: eggs salt

Picture: Hard-boiled eggs worshipping a salt shaker. As they glorify the salt, it is raised into the air, elevated by their praise.

Other forms: Exalted *(adj)*; exaltation *(noun)*

Sentence: The popular queen was *exalted* by all.

EXPUNGE (ex-PUNJ) *verb* — erase

Sounds like: x sponge

Picture: A sponge that erases everything it touches.

Sentence: An asteroid could *expunge* an entire city.

EXTEMPORANEOUS (ex-tem-por-AY-nee-us) *adj* — done without planning; improvised

Sounds like: eggs temp or rains

Picture: You're watching the six o'clock news, waiting for the weather report (you're planning a family back-to-nature camping trip tomorrow and you want to know if you'll need to bring an umbrella for the VCR). But the regular weatherperson is sick and her substitute is this egg who doesn't have a script or any idea what he wants to say. It sounds like this: "If we look at the map, we see a lot of big letters and numbers. Let's see, what do you suppose this "82" means? It could be the temp. Or, the chance of rain, or the amount of rain we might get tonight. Hey, let's all just wait and see what happens. No point in standing here trying to guess what the weather will do, right? Now back to you, Katie and Bob..."

Other form: Extemporaneously *(adv)*

Sentence: He spoke *extemporaneously*, without notes, for an hour.

EXTOL (ex-TOLE) *verb* — **praise**

Sounds like: eggs toll

Picture: A giant egg working as a toll collector. The driver must praise the egg before he's permitted to pass through the gate.

Other form: Extolment *(noun)*

Sentence: The writer was *extolled* for her creativity.

EXTRANEOUS (ex-TRAY-nee-us) *adj* — **unnecessary; irrelevant**

Sounds like: extra trains

Picture: A small town with a small population and a small train station. Each morning exactly two people wait on the platform. At 8:05, the train pulls into the station, the two passengers board, and the train leaves the empty platform behind. At 8:09 another train arrives, but there's nobody there. At 8:14 another train arrives. At 8:20, still another train pulls into the empty station. This continues all day long, eight trains every hour for the only two people in the whole town who commute to work.

Other forms: Extraneously *(adv)*; extraneousness *(noun)*

Sentence: A good editor will eliminate *extraneous* words and phrases.

EXTRICATE (EX-trik-ate) *verb* — **to free from a trap or difficult situation; to disentangle**

Sounds like: eggs truck Kate

Picture: Kate works on a chicken farm. One day, Kate is loading eggs onto the back of a truck when the driver is attacked by a crazed chicken. Startled, the driver puts the truck into gear and takes off, bouncing at high speed down the dirt road into town. Meanwhile, Kate has fallen headfirst into the back of the truck and has been knocked unconscious, buried beneath boxes of eggs, which have toppled onto her. Arriving at his destination, the driver runs to the back of the eggs truck, discovers Kate, and frees her from her trap. (Kate is angry. To find out what she and the driver say to each other, see PALTRY.)

Sentence: The fox worked for hours to *extricate* itself from the trap.

EXUBERANT (ex-ZOO-burr-ent) *adj* — **uncontrollably joyous**

Sounds like: ex-zoo bear aunt

Picture: A grizzly bear who had left the zoo returns to visit his aunt. When they see each other, they are both very happy, hugging and dancing and singing for many hours.

Other forms: Exuberance *(noun)*; exuberantly *(adv)*

Sentence: The city was *exuberant* after its team won the championship.

43

FALLACIOUS (fuh-LAY-shuss) *adj* — **false; misleading**

Sounds like: full ashes

Picture: Father and son on the lawn in front of the son's house. Dad says, "Be sure to always clean the ashes out of the fireplace." He is unaware that the ashes have filled the fireplace and the entire chimney and are spilling out onto the roof. "Don't worry, Dad," says the young man. "I clean it out every day."

Other forms: Fallacy *(noun);* fallaciously *(adv)*

Sentence: Many claims we believe to be true may, years later, turn out to be *fallacious*.

FASTIDIOUS (fass-TID-ee-uss) *adj* — **difficult to please**

Sounds like: fast hideous

Picture: A decorator showing her client many kinds of wallpaper. Every time she holds up a sample, the client says, "Hideous!" The faster she shows the samples, the faster the client says, "Hideous!"

Other forms: Fastidiousness *(noun);* fastidiously *(adv)*

Sentence: The chef was so *fastidious*, no one could stand to work with him.

FERVOR (FER-ver) *noun* — **strong passion**

Sounds like: fever, or forever

Picture: A young man telling his girlfriend how much he loves her. He speaks with an intensity of passion that seems to have no limits. "Ophelia, my love for you is like a hurricane at sea, wild, uncontrollable! I'm drowning in it! It's swallowing me up, tearing me to pieces, dashing me against the rocks. I am shredded by passion! I am consumed by fever! A fever that will last forever!" (The young woman is shocked: "My goodness, Rudy, it sounds like you should be going out with a nurse.")

Other forms: Fervidness *(noun);* fervidly *(adv)*

Sentence: After the woman's claim of a miraculous cure, the town was swept up by religious *fervor*.

FICKLE (FIK-uhl) *adj* — **lacking loyalty; unpredictably changeable; erratic**

Rhymes with: pickle and nickel

Picture: A little girl and her teacher. The teacher is holding up a picture of a pickle and a picture of a nickel and has asked the girl which she likes better. The girl says she likes pickles better. Then she says she likes nickels better. She continues to alternate, changing her mind every few seconds.

Other form: Fickleness *(noun)*

Sentence: Audiences are *fickle*, which is why many celebrities fade from view.

FLACCID (FLASS-id) *adj* — **lacking firmness; soft; limp**

Sounds like: flat Sid

Picture: A jellyfish named Sid. Like all jellyfish, Sid has no bones in his body, so he is unable to maintain any shape. When he's dropped onto a table, he becomes completely flat.

Other forms: Flaccidly *(adv);* flaccidity *(noun)*

Sentence: After months away from the gym, the weightlifter's arms had become *flaccid*.

FLAGRANT (FLAY-grent) *adj* — **openly and obviously evil; glaring; conspicuous**

Looks like: flag rent

Picture: A man and woman parading on the sidewalk in front of their apartment building. Each carries a flag that says, "We have no complaints about this building or our apartment, but we aren't going to pay our rent and we don't care who knows it."

Other forms: Flagrantly *(adv);* flagrancy *(noun)*

Sentence: The attack was a *flagrant* violation of the treaty.

FLEDGLING (FLEJ-ling) *noun* — **beginner**

Sounds like: fresh wings

Picture: A newly-hatched bird trying to fly with fresh wings. He's a beginner.

Sentence: The *fledgling* pilot flew solo for the first time.

FLIPPANCY (FLIP-an-see) *noun* — **treating a serious situation with arrogant humor or disrespect**

Sounds like: flip and see

Picture: A man sits in the electric chair. Just minutes earlier, a storm knocked out power and now one of the guards asks if the electricity is back on. The prisoner smiles casually and gestures to the large switch on the wall next to the chair: "Just flip and see."

Other forms: Flippant *(adj);* flippantly *(adv)*

Sentence: Hal's *flippant* attitude after his arrest only angered the police more.

FOMENT (foe-MENT) *verb* — **to stir into action; rouse; incite**

Sounds like: foam mint

Picture: A man who has covered his face with foam mint (a mint-scented shave cream). He runs through the streets, trying to stir the other men to follow his lead and finally shave off their beards. "It's time to unite," he yells, "and remove the whiskers that keep us from seeing who we really are!"

Other form: Fomentation *(noun)*   Note: Don't confuse with: "ferment," which is a chemical process.

Sentence: The college student was arrested and accused of trying to *foment* a riot.

FORESIGHT (FOR-site) *noun* — **the ability to see ahead, anticipate, or predict**

Sounds like: four sight

Picture: A woman who wakes up each morning at four o'clock with a vision in which she can see the events of the coming day. "I can yell at my kids for things they haven't even thought about doing yet!"

Other forms: Foresighted *(adj);* foresee *(verb)*

Sentence: Even though it was a sunny morning, she had the *foresight* to take an umbrella to work.   45

FRUGAL (FROO-gull) adj
— **careful with money; thrifty**

Sounds like: few gulls

Picture: The man who wasted his inheritance on gulls (see PRODIGAL) has a brother. This brother received the same inheritance, but when he met the seagull salesman, he bought only a few gulls.

Other forms: Frugality (noun); frugally (adv)

Sentence: A *frugal* shopper will wait for sales before buying.

I DON'T CARE WHO PUTS THEIR HAND OUT... WE'RE NOT FORKING OVER ONE MORE DIME!

COAT CHECK

FULMINATE (FULL-min-ate) verb
— **to explode, either with sound or anger**

Sounds like: full men ate

Picture: Three large men at a picnic. They ate and ate until they were full, then the full men ate some more, until they literally exploded. After witnessing this, the men's wives blew up in anger.

Other form: Fulmination (noun)

Sentence: He *fulminated* against his error-prone employee.

FURTIVE (FER-tiv) adj — **sneaky; secretive**

Sounds like: fur tip

Picture: Husband and wife are about to leave a fancy restaurant. They have just picked up her fur from the coat check room and he's complaining about the prices of the meals, the fact that they have to pay for parking, the cost of the babysitter, etc. Meanwhile, his wife is sneaking back to the coat check girl to slip her a dollar.

Other forms: Furtiveness (noun); furtively (adv)

Sentence: Three hours late, he tiptoed *furtively* into the house.

FUTILE (FYOO-til) adj — **hopelessly ineffective; useless; in vain**

Sounds like: few tile

Picture: Two men on a roof. They're professional roofers, which is why they're up there and which means they're supposed to know how to estimate how many tiles they'll need to do a certain roof. But they underestimated and now they're trying to figure out how to stretch the few tiles they have left to cover about forty square feet of roof area. "It's hopeless," says one. "Too few tiles."

NFRTHRMPF MSDSMNR THMPF

Other forms: Futility (noun); futilely (adv)

Sentence: The cow tried to fly, but it was a *futile* effort.

GARBLED (GAR-bulled) adj — **changed so much that the original meaning has been distorted; scrambled**

Sounds like: gargled

Picture: A man talking and gargling at the same time. His friend is trying hard to understand the message, but it's too distorted to comprehend.

Other form: Garble (verb)

Sentence: The email came through, but it was *garbled*.

GARISH (GAIR-ish) *adj* — **flashy; gaudy**

Looks like: car fish

Picture: A fish swimming in the ocean. This fish has fins like a '58 Chevy, with flashy chrome trim and pinstriping; its scales are two-tone metallic. When it moves past other fish, it turns on a set of blinking lights that act as turn signals, and sounds a horn that plays the theme from "Flipper."

Other forms: Garishly *(adv);* garishness *(noun)*

Sentence: In an effort to look exotic, the fortune teller wore a lot of *garish* jewelry.

GARNER (GARR-ner) *verb* — **collect; gather; accumulate; earn**

Sounds like: gardener

Picture: A gardener showing the many ribbons she has collected for her prize-winning flowers.

Sentence: His songs have *garnered* many awards.

GENIAL (JEE-nee-ul) *adj* — **friendly; gracious; kind**

Sounds like: Genie Al

Picture: A Genie named Al has just come out of his bottle. He is extremely friendly and accommodating, wanting very much to please everyone around him.

Other form: Geniality *(noun)*

Sentence: I try to be *genial*, but my natural grouchiness inevitably comes through.

GARRULOUS (GAIR-uh-luss) *adj* — **very talkative; loquacious**

Sounds like: Gary Loose

Think of: A talkative man named Gary Loose Lips. Gary can't stop talking for a second. He wears a pair of low gray shoes, which are also talking (see LOQUACIOUS).

Other form: Garrulity *(noun)*

Sentence: Paul was *garrulous*, so he was a natural choice to be the spokesperson.

GERMANE (jer-MAYNE) *adj* — **relevant; fitting**

Looks like: Germany

Picture: A courtroom. The lawyer asks the witness on the stand, "What's the capital of Germany?" The judge interrupts: " I don't see how that question is relevant to this case. It's not germane."

Sentence: When writing an essay, focus on the *germane* points.

SO WHEN IS THE BABY DUE?

NINE MONTHS OR NINE FEET AROUND, WHICHEVER COMES FIRST

GIRTH (GERTH) *noun* — **distance around an object; circumference**

Rhymes with: birth

Picture: A pregnant woman, very wide around the middle.

Sentence: The old oak tree had a *girth* of twelve feet.

47

GLUTTON (GLUT-tin) *noun* — **a person who consumes huge quantities of food or drink; someone with great endurance**

Looks like: a combination of "glue" and "button"

Picture: A big casserole of glue and buttons. Someone at the dinner table is devouring an enormous amount of this stuff, for some reason.

Other forms: Gluttony *(noun)*; gluttonous *(adj)*

Sentence: His *gluttony*, especially for sweets, got him into a serious medical condition.

GREGARIOUS (greh-GAIR-ee-uss) *adj* — **sociable; extroverted; enjoying companionship**

Sounds like: Greg, Gary, and us

Picture: A man and woman are getting ready to leave for vacation. As the husband carries his suitcase down the stairs, he sees that two friends are seated in his living room. His wife explains that she's invited everyone they know to go on vacation with them. "Well, so far it's Greg, Gary, and us," she says. "But I'm still waiting to hear from Audrey, Fred, and Nora Jean. And Fred's going to call his brother, and Audrey's asking everyone in her building..."

Other form: Gregariousness *(noun)*

Sentence: *Gregarious* people probably make better salesmen.

GULLIBLE (GULL-ih-bull) *adj* — **easily deceived**

Sounds like: gully bull

Picture: A bull has fallen into a gully, tricked by the other bulls.

Other form: Gullibility *(noun)*

Sentence: Don't be so *gullible* that you believe everything.

GRAVITY (GRAH-vih-tee) *noun* — **seriousness**

Sounds exactly like: gravity, the force that holds us to the Earth.

Picture: An astronaut has landed on some distant planet with very powerful gravity. The force is so strong that the astronaut has been flattened by it (a serious situation).

Other forms: Grave *(adj)*; gravely *(adv)*

Sentence: A situation's *gravity* can sometimes cause nervous laughter.

HACKNEYED (HAK-need) *adj* — **unoriginal; trite**

Sounds like: hat kneed

Picture: Two women with fancy hats on their knees commenting on a third woman with baseball caps on her knees.

Sentence: Avoid *hackneyed* phrases in your writing.

HAMPER (HAM-purr) *verb* — **interfere with movement or progress**

Sounds like: hamper (as in clothes hamper)

Picture: A gigantic clothes hamper parked in the middle of a highway, causing traffic to back up for miles.

Sentence: The blizzard *hampered* the search for survivors.

HAPHAZARD (hap-HAZ-erd) *adj* — **without plan or direction**

Sounds like: hop Hazel (also notice the word "hazard")

Picture: Hazel plans to hop across the state of North Dakota. As she gets ready to go, a reporter asks what her plan is, how many maps she has, and how she intends to deal with the hazards out there. Hazel: "Plans? Maps? Who needs them? I'm just going. If I get lost, I'll go a different way. And if I run into any hazards, I'll hop around them. Well, here I go. See you when I get somewhere."

Other forms: Haphazardly *(adv)*; haphazardness *(noun)*

Sentence: Martin planted the trees *haphazardly*, scattering them around the yard.

HARANGUE (her-RANG) *noun* — **a long, lecturing speech**

Sounds like: her gang

Picture: A meeting of a women's gang. The leader is delivering an endless lecture about the importance of wearing helmets on the road. (One member interrupts: "But we're driving stationwagons.")

Other form: Harangue *(verb)*

Sentence: We began wearing earplugs at work to get some relief from his *harangues*.

HARBOR (HAR-ber) *verb* — **to provide shelter or refuge; hide**

Sounds exactly like: harbor (the body of water)

Picture: While fishermen prowl around on the ocean, an organization called "The Undersea Railroad," run by large turtles and seals, helps get fish into the harbor, where they can hide until it's safe.

Sentence: *Harboring* a known criminal is a crime in itself.

HARDY (HARD-ee) *adj* — **bold; brave; capable of withstanding harsh conditions**

Looks like: hard Y

Picture: The letters of the alphabet are in a log cabin, holding a contest to see who can stand out in the cold for the longest time. Now 25 of them have come in to sit near the fire. Several letters are looking out the window at the Y, standing in the snow. It's below zero and windy, but Y doesn't move. "He is one hard letter," says R. "Hey, U, why don't you go out there and tell him to come in?" "Not me," answers U. "We vowels are too soft for this kind of weather."

Other forms: Hardiness *(noun)*; hardily *(adv)*   Don't confuse with "hearty," which means "enthusiastic."

Sentence: Lewis and Clark were *hardy* explorers of rugged terrain.

HEDGE (HEJ) *verb* — **to avoid giving a clear answer, thereby escaping responsibility or blame**

Sounds exactly like: hedge

Picture: A wealthy woman is questioning her gardener about the horribly trimmed hedge in front of her mansion. The gardener, not wishing to be castigated, avoids the question with vague answers: "The hedge? I don't recall who trimmed it this week. I mean, yes, I am the only gardener, but maybe one of the neighborhood kids sneaked into the toolshed and used the clippers. I'm not saying that's what happened, but then again, who can know for sure...?"

Note: "Hedge" means to beat around the bush!

Sentence: Connected to the lie detector, Big Nick tried to *hedge* his way through the test.

HEED (HEED) *verb* — **notice; pay attention to**

Sounds exactly like: he'd

Picture: A boy is about to leave for college. His mother is trying to hide her sadness with an endless string of warnings (addressed to her husband): "He'd better drive carefully. And he'd better call the minute he gets there. And he'd better be listening to me. And he'd better brush his teeth after dinner. And he'd better go to bed early tonight. That's all I'm going to say, but he'd better pay attention. And he'd better study every day. Is he listening to me?"

Other form: Heed *(noun)* — as in, "to take heed."

Sentence: It's wise to *heed* the warnings of a coming hurricane or tornado.

HEINOUS (HAY-niss) *adj* — **shockingly evil**

Sounds like: hang us

Picture: Three men standing on the steps of the gallows, three nooses dangling from the cross-bar. One of the men says to the sheriff, "Our crimes were heinous. All you can do is hang us."

Sentence: An especially *heinous* crime can leave a community in shock for years.

HERESY (HEHR-eh-see) *noun* — **an opinion expressed in defiance of generally accepted ideas**

Sounds like: her a C

Picture: A college philosophy class. Two students are discussing the grade a third student received: "He gave her a C just because she titled her paper, *Socrates Was An Idiot.*"

Other forms: Heretic *(noun);* heretical *(adj)*

Sentence: In centuries past, people were burned at the stake for *heretical* comments.

HIATUS (high-ATE-us) *noun* — **gap; interruption; a break in continuity; a pause**

Sounds like: Hi, Atus

Picture: A group of bricklayers building a wall. As the foreman, a man named Atus, inspects the five-foot-high wall, he comes to a gap — a place where the wall is only a foot high, as if the bricklayer assigned to that portion had stopped working several hours ago. Just then he hears someone yell out, "Hi, Atus!" and turns around to find the missing bricklayer lying down on a lounge chair. The brick layer explains, "I needed a little break."

Sentence: Some companies take a summer *hiatus*, closing down completely for weeks.

HIERARCHY (HY-er-ar-kee) *noun* — **a group of people in authority, ranked in order of power; a sequential listing**

Sounds like: hire Archie

Picture: The executive board meeting of a large corporation. The chairman is standing at a flip-chart showing the company's chain of command, beginning with him at the top. Each of the boxes below the chairman on the chart has the name of a vice president or assistant vice president, except one box, which is blank. The chairman is saying, "I want you to hire Archie for this position. I think he'd fit very well into the hierarchy of the company."

Other form: Hierarchical *(adj)*

Sentence: The military is a *hierarchy*: each level is more powerful than the ones below it.

HOMAGE (OMM-ij) *noun* — **respect paid to someone or something; tribute; honor**

Looks like: home age

Picture: A very, very, very old house. The house has been restored to its original appearance and is beautifully decorated. From miles around, real estate agents, historians, and tourists come to visit the old house and show their respect. "I don't even know the home's age," says one visitor, "but I feel I should pay homage to it."

Sentence: We pay *homage* to certain people by putting their images on stamps and currency.

HOMOGENEOUS (ho-mo-JEEN-ee-us) *adj* — **the same throughout; consistent; uniform**

Sounds like: home of genius

Picture: A genius is being studied by a team of scientists. They're trying to determine if anything about her home life has contributed to her amazing mental abilities. When they arrive they find that the home of this genius is remarkably consistent: all of the rooms are exactly the same size, the walls are all the same color, and every piece of furniture is the same height and style. In addition, the light bulbs are all 75 watts, the air is always maintained at 70 degrees, and every book in the house contains exactly 384 pages. "Hmmm," says one of the scientists, "maybe the home of a genius needs to be homogeneous."

Other forms: Homogeneousness *(noun);* homogeneously *(adv)*

Sentence: If you add chocolate syrup to a glass of milk and stir, you'll get a *homogeneous* mixture.

HYPERBOLE (hi-PURR-boe-lee) *noun* — **extreme exaggeration**

Looks like: Hyper Bowl

Think of two things: the use of the word, "hype," meaning to heavily promote something, thus exaggerating its attraction, and football's Super Bowl, which is usually hyped beyond belief. Now combine these two ideas and imagine a "Hyper Bowl," a game that requires the two teams to out-exaggerate each other. The players are lined up, face-to-face. Someone from one side says, "You don't have a chance against us. We won our last game by forty-seven touchdowns." Someone from the other team responds, "By the time we're finished, they'll have to pick you guys out of the grass with tweezers."

Sentence: "I've told you a million times" is an example of *hyperbole*.

51

YOU KNOW I ALWAYS HAVE YOUR BEST INTERESTS IN MIND.

HYPOCRITE (HIP-oh-crit) *noun*
— **an insincere person; one who pretends to have feelings he doesn't really possess**

Sounds like: hippo crit

Picture: A hippopotamus smiling at his friend, even as he steals his wallet.

Other form: Hypocritical *(adj)*

Sentence: Don't be a *hypocrite* -- say what you mean!

IDOLATRY (eye-DOLL-uh-tree) *noun*
— **the worship of objects or people as gods**

Sounds like: a doll, a tree

Picture: People had been coming from all over town, and now they're arriving from other states, to see the man who worships the doll in the tree. He has placed one of his daughter's dolls high up in a maple tree on his front lawn, and every morning at 7 o'clock he kneels on the damp grass and bows before the doll, praying and asking for forgiveness.

Other forms: Idolater *(noun);* idolize *(verb);* idolatrous *(adj)*

Sentence: In Judeo-Christian scripture, *idolatry* is forbidden by the Ten Commandments.

IMBUE (im-BYOO) *verb* — **to fill, as with a strong dye or a strong feeling**

Looks like: I'm blue

Picture: A worker at the dye factory has fallen into the blue vat. When he pulls himself out, his clothes and skin are completely imbued with the dye. "How do you feel?" his co-workers ask. He responds simply, "I'm blue."

Sentence: The speaker *imbued* her audience with powerful feelings of confidence.

IMMINENT (IMM-uh-nint) *adj*
— **about to take place; happening soon**

Sounds like: in a minute

Picture: A farmer and his son discussing the tornado that's supposed to be on its way. The father, listening to the radio: "They say the tornado is imminent. When do you think it will get here?" The son, looking out the window, sees the dark funnel on the horizon. "In a minute," he says.

Other forms: Imminently *(adv);* imminence *(noun)*

Sentence: Another stabbing contraction and the pregnant woman knew the birth was *imminent*.

IMMUTABLE (im-MYOO-tah-bull) *adj*
— **unable to change**

Looks like: a mute table

Picture: Two chairs have been trying, without success, to strike up a conversation with a table. As the table sits silently (mutely), one chair says to the other, "It's no use. Tables just don't talk. They never have and I guess they never will."

Other forms: Immutability *(noun);* immutably *(adv)*

Sentence: The speed of light seems to be an *immutable* law of nature.

IMPAIR (im-PARE) *verb* — **weaken in strength or value**

Looks like: I'm pair

Picture: An exhausted pear seated at his desk, holding a lamp and talking into it.

Other forms: Impairment *(noun)*; impaired *(adj)*

Sentence: Ed's concentration was *impaired* by alcohol.

IMPASSE (IM-pass) *noun* — **a situation from which you cannot escape; stalemate**

Sounds like: him pass

Picture: Two cars face each other, front-bumper-to-front-bumper, on a narrow road. There isn't enough room for them to go around each other, and neither driver is willing to back up, so they sit. An observer on the side of the road watches the conflict, listening to each driver yell, "I refuse to let *him pass!*"

Don't confuse with: Impassive. Sentence: The two sides reached an *impasse* and negotiations were halted.

IMPASSIVE (im-PASS-iv) *adj* — **without feeling; expressionless**

Looks like: Impasse (refer to the situation described under IMPASSE, above)

Picture: The person watching the impasse between the two drivers is looking on impassively. He is totally unconcerned with how the conflict will be resolved and, as the drivers grow angrier and angrier, he remains calm and expressionless (impassive).

Other forms: Impassively *(adv)*; impassivity *(noun)*

Sentence: Strangely calm, Margaret watched *impassively* as her car rolled into the river.

IMPEDE (im-PEED) *verb* — **get in the way; hinder**

Looks like: I'm Pete

Picture: Pete walks out onto the track while a women's relay race is going on. Just as two racers are about to exchange the baton, he walks between them and says to one, "I'm Pete."

Other form: Impediment *(noun)* Sentence: In baseball, a fielder may not *impede* the progress of a runner.

IMPETUOUS (im-PETCH-oo-us) *adj* — **taking sudden action; hasty; impulsive**

Sounds like: in pet shoes

Picture: Wife comes home with the family sheepdog. Husband is watching TV and looks over to see that the dog is wearing very stylish shoes on all four paws. "I just bought them without thinking," wife explains. "They were there in the window, we were walking by, we both liked them, so I bought them. I know it was impetuous, but hey, he does have that kennel dance next Friday."

Other forms: Impetuosity *(nouns)*; impetuously *(adv)*   Don't confuse with: Impetus

Sentence: People who think before they act may look upon the *impetuous* with curiosity.   53

IMPOSTOR (im-POSS-ter) *noun* — **pretender**

Looks like: I'm Postor

Picture: A man named Mr. Postor is about to receive a special award that includes a $25,000 prize, many gifts, and the praise and respect of thousands of people. Suddenly, another man bursts into the room yelling, "Wait! I'm Postor! He's a fake!"

Sentence: There are many *impostors* lurking on the Internet, so watch out!

IMPUDENCE (IMP-yoo-dense) *noun* — **rudeness; insolence**

Sounds like: in pew dance (a pew is a seat or bench in a church)

Picture: It's Sunday morning and the church is filled. The minister is about to begin her sermon when suddenly a man jumps up in his pew and performs a wild dance. The churchgoers are shocked, to say the least, at his rudeness and lack of consideration for others.

Other forms: Impudent *(adj)*; impudently *(adv)*

Note: Don't confuse with "imprudence," which means "a lack of wisdom" (see PRUDENT).

Sentence: *Impudence*, or any disrespectful behavior, is not tolerated in a court of law.

INADVERTENT (in-ad-VER-tent) *adj* — **unintentional**

Sounds like: in at her tent

Picture: An army troop camping out during an overnight hike. One of the men accidentally walks into the tent of a female officer. Furious, she throws him out. (One observer: "So he made a mistake. What's the big deal?" Second observer: "It's the seventh time today he's made that mistake.")

Other form: Inadvertently *(adv)*

Sentence: The newspaper *inadvertently* switched the names under the picture.

INANE (in-NANE) *adj* — **silly; insignificant**

Looks like: insane (without the "S")

Picture: A man reads a letter from his psychiatrist, then cries to his wife: "He says I'm insane!" When he becomes hysterically upset, she takes the letter and reads it. "No, it says 'inane,'" she tells him. "It's nothing to worry about. You're just being silly."

Other forms: Inanity *(noun)*; inanely *(adv)*

Sentence: It's hard to believe that grown men could argue over such *inane* matters.

INAUGURATE (in-AWG-yer-ate) *verb* — **begin; induct into**

Sounds like: in Aug. you're eight

Picture: The Mid-Childhood Club, made up of children between the ages of eight and thirteen. The president is speaking to a new group of kids, all of whom will be celebrating their 8th birthday on August 1st. The date is July 31: "In Aug. you're eight, and each of you will be officially welcomed into the Mid-Childhood Club."

Other forms: Inauguration *(noun)*; inaugural *(adj)*

Sentence: The President of the United States is *inaugurated* on January 20.

INCESSANT (in-SESS-ent) *adj* — **continuous; endless**

Sounds like: in says ant

Picture: An ant hill just before a storm. One ant stands at the door and says, "In! In! In!" over and over and over as an endless stream of ants pours into the shelter.

Other forms: Incessantly *(adv)*; incessancy *(noun)*

Sentence: The *incessant* buzzing of mosquitoes drove us crazy.

INCHOATE (ink-OH-ett) *adj* — **not yet fully developed**

Sounds like: ink oh-eight

Picture: A tank, such as one you would see at a winery. But this is an inkery, where ink is made and stored. The ink in one particular tank has not aged enough, so is not yet ready for use. The tank is labeled, "Ink 0-8."

Sentence: The *inchoate* army needs a great deal more training.

INCITE (in-SITE) *verb* — **arouse to action; stir up; foment**

Sounds like: ignite

Picture: A small country that has been controlled by a foreign nation for many years. One day, on the tenth anniversary of the country's takeover, a woman runs through the streets of the capital. She calls for action, urging the citizens to fight for their freedom. Like a spark falling into dry grass, she *ignites* a fire of anger among the people, and it quickly grows into a blazing revolution.

Other forms: Incitement, incitation *(nouns)*

Note: Don't confuse with "insight," the ability to perceive.

Sentence: The angry miner *incited* his co-workers to strike.

INCOMPATIBLE (in-kum-PAT-a-bull) *adj* — **incapable of existing together in peace**

Sounds like: in combat with Bill

Picture: A woman has left her husband and gone to stay with a friend. "It's no use," she says. "Every day I find myself in combat with Bill. We just cannot get along."

Other forms: Incompatibility *(noun)*; incompatibly *(adv)*

Sentence: Very often, two male animals are *incompatible*.

INCONGRUOUS (in-KON-groo-uss) *adj* — **out of place**

Sounds like: in Congress

Picture: The U.S. Capitol (Congress) with something unexpected in the middle of the picture.

Other forms: Incongruity *(noun)*; incongruously *(adv)*

Sentence: A tuxedo would be *incongruous* at the beach.

INCORRIGIBLE (in-KORR-ij-uh-bull) *adj* — **impossible to correct, control, or discipline**

Sounds like: in car itch a bull

Picture: A bull family out for a drive in their Ford Taurus. One of the children in the back seat has put fleas and ticks under his father's seat. The father, trying to drive, is squirming from the itch. Mother Bull scolds her son: "You are absolutely incorrigible!"

Other forms: Incorrigibility *(noun);* incorrigibly *(adv)*

Sentence: Those prisoners deemed *incorrigible* are often separated from the others.

INCREDULOUS (in-CREJ-oo-luss) *adj* — **unwilling or unable to believe**

Sounds like: ink red, you lose!

Picture: A man is playing roulette at a casino. He's been at it a while, winning, losing, winning, losing. Now he's put all of his money, including his car keys and the deed to his house, on "25 Black." The attendant spins the wheel and talks as the wheel slows down: "looking for black ink, looking for black ink, looking for black... and ink's red, you lose!" The man stares at the wheel for a long time. "I can't believe it," he says. "I just can't believe it!"

Other forms: Incredulity *(noun);* incredulously *(adv)*

Note: An object or event is *incredible*; the person observing it is *incredulous*. Also, connect with other words containing the root "cred," such as credence, credulous, credibility, credentials, and credit; all have to do with "belief."

Sentence: He watched *incredulously* as his dog got into the family minivan and drove away.

INDICT (in-DITE) *verb* — **charge with a crime; accuse**

Sounds like: in tight

Picture: A man has his right arm stuck in the cash slot of an automated teller machine at the bank. An alarm has sounded and the police are about to come in. "I'm really in tight here," he thinks. "I'm sure they're going to charge me with attempted robbery."

Other form: Indictment *(noun)*

Sentence: The gangster was *indicted* on four counts of murder.

INDIGENT (INN-deh-jint) *adj* — **very poor**

Sounds like: Indy Gent

Picture: A very poor man named Indy Gent. His clothes are tattered and dirty and he has few or no possessions.

Other forms: Indigence, indigent *(nouns)*

Note: Don't confuse this word with "indigenous," which means "native or inborn." Or "indignant," which means "angry."

Sentence: Pauline works hard to help the homeless and the *indigent*.

INDOLENT (INN-doe-lent) *adj* — **lazy**

Connect with: Indigent. Picture Indy Gent, who is very poor. Now think of why he's so poor. Maybe he's extremely lazy and doesn't want to work. So he's indigent because he's indolent. To distinguish between the two similar sounding words, remember that indolent has an "L" in it, for lazy.

Other forms: Indolence *(noun)*; indolently *(adv)*

Sentence: Martha was a hard worker and could not tolerate *indolence* in her children.

INDUCE (in-DOOSE) *verb* — **cause to happen; bring about**

Sounds like: in deuce

Picture: Two well-known tennis players are engaged in a long and difficult match. One player falls behind in the final game, then suddenly manages to lure his opponent into a series of mistakes (he's caused the mistakes to happen). Now they're in deuce.

Other forms: Inducement *(noun);* inducible *(adj)*

Sentence: He was a persuasive salesman and could *induce* his customers to buy almost anything.

INERT (ih-NERT) *adj* — **lacking movement; inactive; sluggish**

Sounds like: in dirt

Picture: Fossils of animals found deep in the dirt. They have remained motionless and unchanged for many thousands of years. They are inert.

Other forms: Inertness, inertia *(nouns);* inertly *(adv)*

Sentence: The Dark Ages are typically portrayed as a time of cultural *inertness*.

INFALLIBLE (in-FAHL-ih-bull) *adj* — **incapable of making a mistake**

Looks like: in fall a bell

Picture: A tall tower in the middle of town. In the tower there is a bell that rings just once a year, at the moment summer ends and fall begins. Whether the season starts on September 20, 21, or 22, the bell always rings exactly on schedule, to the second. It never makes a mistake.

Other forms: Infallibility *(noun);* infallibly *(adv)*   Alternate approach: Just think of "in*fail*able."

Sentence: An *infallible* system for predicting numbers would spell the end of all lotteries.

INFAMY (INN-fuh-mee) *noun* — **a bad reputation; notoriety**

Sounds like: in for me

Picture: A lifelong criminal is complaining about the news media. "They've got it in for me," he says. "And why? What have I done? Some bank robberies, two or three dozen murders, a kidnapping here and there. So where did I get this terrible reputation?"

Other form: Infamous *(adj)*   Sentence: Some criminals seek immortality by living on in *infamy*.

INFER (in-FER) *verb* — **to figure out, based on given information; conclude; deduce**

Sounds like: in fur

Picture: A scientist finds a baby seal on the shore and notices that the seal's fur is coated with oil. From this information (the oil in the fur), the scientist concludes that there has been an oil spill in the area.

Other form: Inference *(noun)*   Note: Infer doesn't mean "to imply" or "to suggest." When you infer something, you *take in* information.

Sentence: We can *infer* from his casual dress that he didn't read the invitation carefully.

INFILTRATE (IN-fil-trayt) *verb* — **penetrate by passing through gaps; enter secretly and become established, such as a spy might do in an enemy organization**

Sounds like: infield rate

Picture: The owner of a major league baseball team is upset. Someone has leaked to the press very secret information about what she's paying the infielders on the team (infield rate). "There's a spy among us," she tells her board of directors. "Someone has infiltrated this organization and is telling our financial business to the newspapers. Now all the outfielders will want raises."

Other form: Infiltration *(noun)*   Sentence: Intelligence agencies try to *infiltrate* enemy organizations.

INGENUOUS (in-JEN-yoo-us) *adj* — **naive; unsophisticated; inexperienced**

Looks like: ingenious

Remember: "Ingenuous" and "ingenious" look almost exactly alike, so it's easy to confuse them. Take a good long look at both words. Learn to distinguish between them. (In a sense, they're opposites.)

Now, imagine a brilliant person, such as Thomas Edison, who has come up with an *ingenious* invention, such as the light bulb. Now also imagine that Mr. Edison is pretty unsophisticated, or *ingenuous*, when it comes to business. He might say something like, "Okay, so it lights up. Big deal. Who's going to buy it? Everyone has candles. Maybe I'll just give it to my cousin Phil, and if he wants to market it, let him make a few bucks." Mrs. Edison replies, "Tom, you're so ingenious, but you're also ingenuous."

Other forms: ingenuousness *(noun);* ingenuously *(adv)* Connect with: Disingenuous ("shrewd")

Sentence: His *ingenuous* manner led us to believe he was incapable of deceit.

INNATE (in-NATE) *adj* — **having a quality that arises from within, rather than learned or acquired from the outside; native; inborn**

Sounds like: Inn Eight

Picture: A woman and man are looking through a guidebook in search of a country inn for their vacation. "I like inn number eight," says the woman, pointing at a number on a map in the book. "It doesn't have a swimming pool, or a fancy menu, or a golf course nearby. But there seems to be something about this place. It has an innate quality, a charm the others are missing."

Other forms: Innateness *(noun);* innately *(adv)*   Note: Be careful not to confuse "innate" with "inane."

Sentence: Elephants have an *innate* tendency to stick together and help each other.

INNOCUOUS (in-NOK-yoo-uss) *adj*
— **harmless; inoffensive**

Sounds like: inn octopus

Picture: A couple arriving for a weekend stay at a country inn. The innkeeper points out the dining room, the fireplace in the library, and the live octopus in the parlor. "Don't worry about him," the host says to the startled guests. "He's harmless."

Other form: Innocuously *(adv)*

Sentence: The drink looked *innocuous,* but actually contained a deadly poison.

INNOVATION (in-no-VAY-shun) *noun*
— **a new idea, product, or method**

Sounds like: an ovation

Picture: An inventor talking to the producer of a TV show. He has invented a device that simulates the sound of a crowd giving an ovation. The producer considers it a great innovation, because it eliminates the need for live people, who could be unpredictable in their responses to the show.

Other forms: Innovative *(adj);* innovate *(verb)*

Sentence: The twentieth century was probably the richest period of *innovation* in history.

INSCRUTABLE (in-SKROO-tuh-bull) *adj*
— **mysterious**

Sounds like: on scooter bull

Picture: Archeologists have discovered drawings on the walls of a cave. The drawings are thousands of years old and clearly show a bull riding a scooter. "We shall call these drawings, "On Scooter Bull," says a scientist. "But we may never know what they mean."

Other forms: Inscrutability *(noun);* inscrutably *(adv)*

Sentence: People have always longed to understand the *inscrutable* universe.

INSIPID (in-SIP-id) *adj*
— **dull; flat; without sparkle or flavor**

Sounds like: in! sip it!

Picture: A young child, sick with the flu. Her mother is trying to get her to drink some flat ginger ale to calm the child's upset stomach. "In!" she says. "In! Sip it! I know it has no flavor. Just sip it."

Other form: Insipidly *(adv)*

Sentence: Amy was surprised that her husband could enjoy such a boring, *insipid* movie.

INSOLENT (IN-so-lent) *adj*
— **rude; haughty**

Sounds like: insulin (a hormone produced by the pancreas)

Picture: A meeting of the body's internal organs. Each speaks in turn. Suddenly the pancreas starts yelling about how important he is, and how the body wouldn't be able to absorb carbohydrates without his insulin, and how he should be thanked for the work he does. ("There he goes again," says the liver. "Spouting insulin and insolence. I hope he doesn't get the stomach upset.")

Other forms: Insolence *(noun);* insolently *(adv)*

Sentence: Lenny was suspended from school for his *insolent* behavior.

INSOLVENT (in-SOL-vent) adj
— **unable to pay bills; bankrupt**

Sounds like: in Sol's vent

Picture: The owner of a small business walks to the bank to make a deposit. Right in front of Sol's Ripoff Emporium he trips, dropping the bag of money down a vent in the sidewalk. When he looks down, he sees the bag, but it's now in Sol's basement. Sol is a crook and will never give it back. "All my money's in Sol's vent!" he cries. "Now I won't be able to pay my bills!"

Other form: Insolvency *(noun)*

Sentence: The workers' morale was low because they knew the company was facing *insolvency.*

INTERMITTENT (in-ter-MIT-tint) adj
— **occurring at intervals; periodic; not constant or continual**

Sounds like: in her mitten

Picture: A little girl stands outside in the falling snow. Every once in a while, a snowflake lands in her mitten. She never knows when it will happen, but she knows it will happen again soon.

Other forms: Intermittently *(adv);* intermission *(noun)*

Sentence: The *intermittent* showers were followed by long periods of sunshine.

INTRACTABLE (in-TRACK-tah-bull) adj —
stubborn; immovable

Looks like: in-track table

Picture: A table wedged between railroad tracks. Two people are trying to move it. "It's no use," says one. "It refuses to budge."

Other forms: Intractability *(noun);* intractably *(adv)*

Sentence: Rita was *intractable* in her belief that she'd been abducted by aliens.

INTRINSIC (in-TRIN-zik) adj
— **located within the very nature of an object or person; inherent**

Sounds like: in train sick

Picture: A man and woman on a train. The man looks as if he's about to either throw up or pass out. Meanwhile, his wife explains to the conductor, "No, it isn't the motion or the speed or the noise, because he doesn't get sick on cars or airplanes or roller coasters. There's some quality intrinsic to trains that makes him feel sick."

Other form: Intrinsically *(adv)*

Sentence: Clean water has *intrinsic* value, while antique cars have market value.

INVERT (in-VERT) verb — **turn upside down or inside out; reverse position**

Looks like: invent

Picture: A scientist named Dr. Bert Invert, who has invented a device that turns objects upside down, regardless of their size or weight. When you enter Dr. Invert's lab, you notice that tables, chairs, desks, and lamps are all upside down. "I was going to invert the entire building," he says, "but the plumber advised against it."

Other forms: Inversion *(noun);* inverted and invertible *(adj)*

Sentence: The printer accidentally *inverted* the image on the poster.

60

IRASCIBLE (ihr-RASS-ih-bull) *adj* — **easily angered**

Sounds like: erase a bull

Picture: A very tempermental artist has been trying to draw a bull for several days, but every version looks worse than the one before. As he gets angrier and angrier, he screams at himself, "Draw a bull, erase a bull. Draw a bull, erase a bull!"

Other forms: Irascibleness *(noun);* irascibly *(adv)*

Sentence: He's *irascible* in the morning; don't talk to him before noon.

IRONY (EYE-rah-nee) or (EYE-er-nee) *noun* — **an unexpected outcome, or the use of a word that is the opposite of its literal meaning**

Sounds like: iron knee

Picture: Basketball player who wished for knees like iron. Instead, he got irons on his knees.

Other forms: Ironic *(adj);* ironically *(adv)*

Sentence: It's *ironic* that he tripped on a crutch and broke his leg.

MAYBE IT'LL HELP HIM WITH THE FULL COURT PRESS

IRRESOLUTE (eer-REZ-uh-loot) *adj* — **indecisive; unsure**

Sounds like: ear razor loot

Picture: A man, dressed as a giant ear, in the audience of "Let's Make A Deal." Does he keep the electric razor he's won or go for the loot behind door number 3? "I'll keep the razor. No, wait, I'll take the loot. I don't know, the razor or the loot? How much time do I have? Can I call you in the morning?"

Other forms: Irresoluteness *(noun) ;* irresolutely *(adv)*

Sentence: His *irresolute* attitude about getting married caused her to call off the wedding.

IRREVERENT (eer-REV-rent) *adj* — **disrespectful**

Sounds like: ear Reverend

Picture: In the lobby of the church hangs a photograph of the Reverend. One of the members of the congregation, obviously lacking in respect for this particular member of the clergy, has painted enormous ears on the Reverend's picture.

Other forms: Irreverence *(noun);* irreverently *(adv)*

Connect with: Revere (opposite)

Sentence: Pamela's *irreverent* remarks got her into trouble with her supervisor.

JARGON (JARR-gun) *noun* — **specialized language used by a particular group**

Sounds like: jar gone

Picture: Policeman questioning the burglary victim: "So you're saying that the alleged perpetrator unlawfully removed from your domicile one wide-mouthed vessel made principally of earthenware?" Victim pointing to empty shelf: "No, what I'm saying is that my jar is gone."

Sentence: The use of *jargon* can be an efficient way to communicate, especially in an emergency.

JAUNDICE (JAWN-diss) *noun* — **yellow color; or, envy or resentment**

Sounds like: enjoying this

Picture: The little third-grade girl couldn't wait for her mother to come to Parents' Night at her school so she could show off her artwork. Everyone in the class had to draw and then paint something yellow. The girl drew pencils and bananas and daffodils, painted them all yellow, wrote "Yellow Stuff" at the top, and taped it to her classroom wall. But when her mother came into the room, she stopped at another girl's work (called "Color My World Yellow") and admired it so much she couldn't tear herself away to look at her daughter's painting. "I'm sorry, dear," the mother said, "but I'm enjoying this. I'll see yours later." The little girl could only look on in envy.

Other form: Jaundiced *(adj)*

Sentence: *Jaundice*, a yellowish look to the skin, may be a sign of liver trouble.

YOU FIND ONE MORE DAILY DOUBLE, PAL, AND I'LL BASH YOUR FACE IN!

I'LL TAKE 'SORE LOSERS' FOR ONE HUNDRED, PLEASE, ALEX

TDP

JAUNTY (JAWN-tee) *adj* — **lively; perky**

Sounds like: jointy

Picture: A wooden puppet dancing around, each of his *joints* swinging freely and rhythmically.

Other forms: Jauntiness *(noun)*; jauntily *(adv)*
Note: Don't confuse with "jaunt" (a short trip).

Sentence: The host's *jaunty* mood soon had everyone enjoying the party.

JEOPARDY (JEP-er-dee) *noun* — **the threat or possibility of danger**

Sounds exactly like: *Jeopardy!* (the TV show)

Picture: The set of the *Jeopardy!* show. The three contestants are standing behind their podiums. Suddenly, the player in the lead finds himself in possible danger because of the resentment of one of his fellow contestants.

Other form: Jeopardize *(verb)*

Sentence: One drunk driver can put many lives in *jeopardy*.

JETTISON (JET-ih-sun) *verb* — **to throw overboard; to discard**

Sounds like: jet a son

Picture: A jet plane ten thousand feet up and running out of fuel. The captain tells the flight attendants to open one of the emergency doors and get rid of all unnecessary cargo in order to make the plane lighter. One of the passengers offers to throw his teenage son out if it would help.

Sentence: The space shuttle *jettisons* its external fuel tanks after launch.

JOCULAR (JOCK-yoo-ler) *adj* — **joking; playful; jesting; witty**

Sounds like: Dracula

Picture: Count Dracula is working as a stand-up comedian, using the name Count Jocular: ("...So he says to me, 'I can't take blood from a stone.' I say, I know, I've been trying for years!")

Other forms: Jocularity *(noun)*; jocularly *(adv)*

Connect with: "Jocose" and "jocund," which have similar meanings to "jocular." Just about any unfamiliar word you come across that begins with "joc" will have something to do with "joke."

Sentence: Her *jocular* personality kept everyone loose during the long flight across the Pacific.

JUBILANT (JOO-bill-ent) *adj* — **filled with joy**

Sounds like: gerbil ant

Picture: A gerbil and an ant are very happy to see each other after a long time. They hug and dance and smile and kiss each other. ("I'm sorry I haven't called," says the gerbil, "but I do about twelve miles a day on that wheel and it really wears me out." "I know what you mean," replies the ant, "I've been working with a bunch of carpenter friends on a wood-frame house a few blocks from here, and that's been keeping me busy for months. But I'm so happy to see you!")

Other forms: Jubilation *(noun)*; jubilantly *(adv)*

Sentence: Rescue workers were *jubilant* when they found someone alive under the rubble.

JUDICIOUS (joo-DISH-uss) *adj* — **wise; making good decisions**

Sounds like: Jew dishes

Picture: Passover is an important holiday for Jewish people. For those who celebrate it in the most traditional way, special dishes are used for the food — dishes that are used only for Passover. Imagine a family that's about to begin the Passover ceremony. The man says to his wife, "I think you made a wise decision by taking out your grandmother's old dishes this year. They make the table look beautiful!"

Other forms: Judiciousness *(noun)*; judiciously *(adv)*

Sentence: Even when there isn't much to do, good employees will make *judicious* use of their time.

JUNCTURE (JUNK-sher) *noun* — **point in time, especially a crucial one; joint or connection**

Sounds like: junk chair

Picture: You are one of seven people playing musical chairs. Everyone is circling the six chairs and the music has just stopped. You look at the two chairs you have stopped between; one looks okay but the other seems to be falling apart. It is time to make a crucial decision: do you take a chance with the junk chair, which is closer, or do you lunge for the sturdier-looking chair?

Sentence: The bombing of Pearl Harbor was a key *juncture* in modern world history.

JUXTAPOSE (juk-stah-POZE) *verb* — to place side-by-side

Sounds like: just suppose

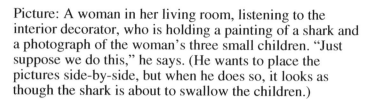

Picture: A woman in her living room, listening to the interior decorator, who is holding a painting of a shark and a photograph of the woman's three small children. "Just suppose we do this," he says. (He wants to place the pictures side-by-side, but when he does so, it looks as though the shark is about to swallow the children.)

Other form: Juxtaposition *(noun)*

Sentence: The *juxtaposition* of sound is important in music.

KINDLE (KIN-dil) *verb* — to start a fire; ignite; arouse

Sounds like: candle

Picture: A young man is serving dinner to his date, who is seated opposite him at an elegant table. He lights one of the candles, hoping the romantic atmosphere will kindle feelings of love in the woman. Instead, he accidentally knocks the candle over onto the tablecloth, kindling a small but disruptive fire.

Sentence: Often it is one special teacher who *kindles* a student's lifelong interest in a subject.

KINETIC (kin-ETT-ik) *adj* — in motion; active

Sounds like: Connecticut

Picture: You're on the space shuttle orbiting the Earth. As you pass over the northeastern United States, you notice the entire region is absolutely still, except in Connecticut, where everything is in motion. Trees are hopping, buildings are sliding from block to block, and mountains are spinning like inverted tops.

Sentence: A falling object has *kinetic* energy.

LACONIC (luh-KONN-ik) *adj* — quiet; of few words; terse

Sounds like: Lake Onnic

Picture: A lake hidden in the woods of Maine, where the birds sing one note at a time. A man rows a boat across the lake; a woman rows her boat from the opposite side. As they pass, he says, "Morning." She replies, "Bye." And so it is on Lake Onnic, where the people keep things inside and say very little.

Sentence: A monastery might be the perfect place for a *laconic* man.

LAMENT (luh-MENT) *verb* — express sorrow; complain

Sounds like: lamb mint

Picture: A flock of sheep has wandered into town, looking for one of their lost members. As they pass a restaurant, they notice "Lamb with Mint Jelly" on the menu. Immediately, their imaginations run wild and they convince themselves that the lamb on the menu is the lamb they've been looking for. Overcome with grief and sorrow, they all sit on the sidewalk in front of the restaurant, moaning and wailing.

Other forms: Lament, lamentation *(nouns);* lamentable *(adj);* lamentably *(adv)*

64   Sentence: The embarrassing incident at the salad bar was simply a *lamentable* mistake.

LANGUISH (LANG-gwish) *verb* — **lose energy or motivation; become weak or depressed**

Sounds like: Lang wish

Picture: A young man named Lang. He graduated from college eight months ago and has been lying around ever since. Every day he says to his dog, lying on the floor next to him, "I wish I could find the energy to go get a job, but I'm just too tired today."

Connect with: Languor *(noun);* languorous *(adj)*

Sentence: The unmotivated team *languished* in last place all season.

LATENT (LAY-tint) *adj*
— **existing but inactive, such as a certain quality; dormant; invisible**

Looks like: Latin

Picture: A woman who learned Latin when she was very young, then ignored it for the next seventy years. Throughout her adult life, Latin words and phrases would occasionally race through her mind and roll around in her mouth, but she would never express them. Her fluency in the language still resided within her, but she stifled it, so that her Latin remained dormant — a latent ability.

Other form: Latency *(noun)*

Sentence: A disease can remain in the body, *latent* and undetected, for years.

LAUD (LAWD) *verb*
— **praise; worship; extol**

Sounds like: lord

Picture: A minister preaching in a church in Alabama. "Laud," he says in his Alabama accent, "you are truly great! Laud, we worship and extol you. Laud, we offer you our praise!"

Other forms: Laudatory, laudable *(adj);* laudably *(adv)*

Sentence: The review was completely *laudatory* -- it didn't contain a single negative comment.

LEGACY (LEGG-uh-see) *noun*
— **something inherited, either from an ancestor or from the past itself**

Sounds like: leg I see

Picture: The nephew is waiting patiently as his uncle's will is being read. Finally it is announced that he has inherited a single leg of an antique chair. "A leg, I see," he says.

Note: A legacy could be a physical gift, such as money, or something abstract, such as knowledge.

Sentence: Her funding of the museum was a *legacy* to future generations.

LETHARGIC (leh-THAR-jik) *adj*
— **tired; sluggish; drowsy**

Sounds like: leather chick

Picture: A young chicken is trying to run around the barn, but she's too tired. The problem is that when she hatched she was covered with leather instead of feathers, and the combination of heat and the weight of the leather has drained her of all her energy.

Other forms: Lethargy *(noun);* lethargically *(adv)*

Sentence: He'd intended to mow the lawn, but was too *lethargic* and simply fell asleep.

LEVITY (LEV-ih-tee) *noun* — **lightness; playfulness; jocularity**

Sounds like: levitate

Picture: A magician is levitating his assistant; that is, he is causing her to float in mid-air without ropes or wires. Normally, magicians are very serious about this part of their act, asking the audience to keep silent, dimming the lights, and behaving as if the assistants were in some sort of danger. However, this particular magician is quite the opposite. As he levitates the young woman, he dances around, smiles, and tells jokes. "Excuse my levity, folks, but I'm just trying to get a *rise* out of her!"

Sentence: Even the most serious films usually have moments of *levity*.

LIONIZE (LIE-uh-nize) *verb* — **to put someone onto a pedestal; to treat with great respect**

Sounds like: lion eyes

Picture: In the jungle, a group of lions has decided to honor a leopard for his courage, strength, and skill. He has what they call "lion eyes," and has therefore been chosen to be an honorary lion, making him a great celebrity in the jungle.

Sentence: Abraham Lincoln is now *lionized* by members of all political parties.

LISTLESS (LIST-less) *adj* — **tired; sluggish; lacking drive**

Sounds exactly like: list less

Picture: Doctor speaking to a tired-looking patient: "When did you start feeling this way?" The patient replies, "I found this list in a magazine, 'Ten Ways to Stay Energetic.' But I lost the list last week, and I've been exhausted ever since."

Other forms: Listlessness *(noun);* listlessly *(adv)*

Sentence: People who have trouble sleeping are often *listless* during the day.

LOATH (LOATH) *adj* — **reluctant; unwilling**

Sounds like: load

Picture: You've just finished watering and combing your prize-winning lawn. A dump truck filled with rocks and boulders pulls up in front of your house. The driver gets out and tells you that he's supposed to dump the load onto your lawn. You, of course, are loath to let him do so.

Sentence: Nancy loved her kids, but she was *loath* to eat the breakfast they'd made for her.

LOATHE (LOATH) *verb* — **to hate**

Sounds exactly like: loath

So how do you tell "loath" and "loathe" apart? It's easy: just look at the end of the word "loathe," which means "to hate." Loathe has the letters H-A-T-E in it (they're jumbled a bit, but they're there). So if you can spell hate, that's what it means.

     Other forms: Loathsomeness, loathing *(nouns);* loathsome *(adj);* loathsomely *(adv)*

     Sentence: Crimes against children are considered *loathsome*, even among other criminals.

LOFTY (LAWF-tee) *adj* — **at a great height; elevated; noble**

Sounds like: loft tea

Picture: A 50-story building. At the very top is a loft, being used by a group of philosophers for a daily tea party. On the street, a man sweeps the sidewalk and talks to a passerby, who is looking up toward the loft. "They're up there drinking fancy tea," says the man, "and discussing their lofty ideas."

Other form: Loftiness *(noun)*   Sentence: He was well into his eighties, yet he still had *lofty* goals.

LOQUACIOUS (low-QUAY-shuss) *adj* — **talkative**

Sounds like: low gray shoes

Picture: A pair of low gray shoes; both are talking.

Other forms: Loquaciousness *(noun)*; loquaciously *(adv)*

Sentence: The *loquacious* lady in the library irritated those trying to read.

LUCID (LOO-sid) *adj* — **easy to understand; transparent; clear-thinking**

Sounds like: Lou said

Picture: A lecture, featuring a speaker named Lou, has just ended. As members of the audience leave the auditorium, one of them can be heard to say, "I understood everything Lou said. It was all so clear."

Other forms: Lucidity *(noun)*; lucidly *(adv)*

Sentence: Jerome was surprisingly *lucid* for someone who had just fallen on his head.

LUDICROUS (LOO-dih-kruss) *adj* — **absurd; ridiculous**

Sounds like: Lou to cross

Picture: A 24-lane super highway. Cars are racing by at 80 mph in every lane. Lou stands at the edge of the highway, waiting for a break in the traffic so he can cross. "Lou," yells a friend from a passing car, "it's ludicrous to think you can ever get across. There hasn't been a break in this traffic since 1986!" ("Well, isn't that ludicrous?" Lou says. "Does that guy really think I can hear him with all these cars going by?")

Other forms: Ludicrousness *(noun)*; ludicrously *(adv)*

Sentence: It's *ludicrous* to say second-hand smoke is harmless.

LUGUBRIOUS (loo-GOOB-ree-uss) *adj* — **mournful**

Sounds like: Lou Goober's

Picture: Lou Goober's Funeral Home. Lou is a sad-looking guy.

Other forms: Lugubriousness *(noun)*; lugubriously *(adv)*

Sentence: *Lugubrious* music saturated the funeral service.

67

MAGNANIMOUS (mag-NAN-ih-muss) *adj* — **big-hearted; generous; forgiving; noble**

Sounds like: my Nanny Moose

Picture: Young moose telling her classmates about her grandma, Nanny Moose, "the most generous, wonderful, kind-hearted moose in the whole world."

Other forms: Magnanimously *(adv)*; magnanimity *(noun)* Note that the root "magn" means great or large, while "anim" pertains to the mind, soul, or spirit. Thus, big-hearted.

Sentence: Even after ten years in prison as an innocent man, he was *magnanimous* upon his release.

MAGNATE (MAG-net) *noun* — **a person of great power**

Sounds like: magnet

Picture: A country populated by paper clips and other small, metal objects. The country's ruler is a large, powerful magnet. The magnet has total influence and control over the citizens.

Sentence: A billionaire real estate *magnate*, he owned a quarter of the town.

The root "mal" means "bad." For the next four words, we will examine the words and actions of a most unpleasant person. His name is Mal.

MALEDICTION (mal-uh-DIK-shun) *noun* — **evil speech; curse**

Sounds like: Mal eviction

Picture: Mal hasn't paid his rent in five months and has received an eviction notice. The letter explains that he must either pay all back rent within 30 days or be kicked out of his apartment. Furious, he calls his landlady on the phone and screams and curses at her, and calls her horrible names.

Other form: Maledictory *(adj)*

Sentence: When angered, he could be a fountain of unkind thoughts and *malediction*.

MALEFACTOR (mal-uh-FAK-ter) *noun* — **person who tries to hurt others; criminal**

Sounds like: Mal he faxed her

Picture: Mal is still upset about the eviction notice (see MALEDICTION) and plans to send his landlady a letter bomb. But instead of mailing the letter bomb, he decides to fax it to her. Of course, she receives a harmless letter, the fax machine blows up in Mal's face, and he grows even angrier (see MALICE).

Other form: Malefaction *(noun)*

Sentence: She'd hoped he would be a benefactor, but he turned out to be the opposite -- a *malefactor*.

MALICE (MAL-iss) *noun* — a desire to cause harm or suffering

Looks like: Mal ice

Picture: Mal is on the roof of his building with a gigantic block of ice, which he's about to drop onto his landlady's head.

Other forms: Malicious (adj); maliciously *(adv)*

Sentence: He wasn't just mean; he was *malicious*.

MALIGN (muh-LINE) *verb* — to say evil or harmful things about someone; defame; vilify

Sounds like: Mal lying

Picture: Mal's landlady has taken him to court for non-payment of rent. On the witness stand, Mal pretends to be an innocent victim. Instead of fighting, he decides to malign his landlady by lying about her. He says that she called him up and said horrible things to him on the phone, faxed him a letter bomb, and even tried to drop a block of ice on his head.

Other form: Malignant *(adj)*

Sentence: He was so angered to learn the tumor was *malignant*, he *maligned* the entire hospital staff.

MALLEABLE (MAL-ee-uh-bull) *adj* — able to be reshaped by force; pliable; impressionable

Sounds like: mallet-able

Picture: A woman who collects sculpture, but whose taste in art changes every day. After purchasing dozens of sculptures, only to quickly grow tired of them, she decides to buy one made of raw clay. She also goes to the hardware store and gets herself a mallet (little hammer). Now, when she gets bored with the sculpture's shape, she beats it with the hammer until it looks like something else. "It may not be marketable as art," she says, "but it sure is malleable."

Other form: Malleability *(noun)*

Sentence: She enjoyed working with younger students, while their minds were still *malleable*.

MARRED (MARD) *adj* — spoiled, scratched, blemished

Sounds like: Mars

Picture: The surface of Mars, which is pitted with craters.

Other form: Mar *(verb)*

Sentence: The new table arrived on time, but was *marred* by scratches and dents.

MEAGER (MEE-ger) *adj* — small in size or amount; thin; weak

Sounds like: me grrr

Picture: A small, frail puppy has just been given his bowl, which contains a tiny amount of food. As gigantic human feet walk by, the puppy expresses his anger over the meager dinner: "Me grrrr!"

Other forms: Meagerness *(noun);* meagerly *(adv)*

Sentence: The movie promised plenty of action, but the plot was *meager*.

69

MEANDER (me-ANN-der) *verb*
— **wander in a carefree manner;**
follow a winding course; ramble

Sounds like: me and her

Picture: A young man, newly in love, walks down a path along a winding river, his arm around his girlfriend. They walk slowly, mindlessly, he singing a song he makes up as they go along:
"Me and her,
My girl Wanda,
We love to wander,
Me and her..."

Other forms: Meandering *(adj);* meander *(noun)*

Sentence: *Meandering* through the woods without a destination was Nancy's favorite activity.

MELLIFLUOUS (mel-IF-loo-uss) *adj*
— **smooth; sweetly flowing**

Sounds like: Mel leaf loose

Picture: Mel is an opera singer. His voice is so smooth, so sweet, that it makes the trees shiver and lose their leaves. (A man raking the leaves might say: "I never did like opera!")

Other forms: Mellifluously *(adv);* mellifluent *(adj)*

Sentence: Many people enjoy the *mellifluous* sound of water running over rocks.

MENDACITY (men-DAH-sih-tee) *noun* — **a lie; a false statement**

Sounds like: mend a city

Picture: Grandpa and Grandson sitting on the porch. Grandpa is telling one of his famous stories: "It was 1929, I guess. I was living in California, a place called Menda City. Well, one morning an earthquake hit, and I'm talking about a real whopper. Every building was down. People had no place to live, they were living in the streets, businesses had to close. And here I was, the only person in town who knew how to build anything. So I started teaching some of the others and we got to fixing things up. I directed the whole project, which was called 'Operation Mend A City.' Get it? Mend A City. Menda City. See how that worked? Anyway, soon we had all brand new buildings and life got back to normal, and the people were so grateful, they made me mayor and wouldn't let me leave office for the next twenty years..." (Grandson thinking to himself, "I get sent to my room for telling stories like this.")

Other forms: Mendacious *(adj);* mendaciously *(adv)*

Sentence: Sarah grew tired of Paula's *mendacities* and began to look for a more honest employee.

METICULOUS (meh-TIK-yoo-luss) *adj* — **very careful about details**

Sounds like: me ticklish

Picture: Man who works in a pillow factory. His job is to stuff the feathers into the pillows. He has to be careful because he's very ticklish and if he doesn't do his job exactly right, he ends up on the floor, laughing. ("But if I do a good job," he says, "I get to take a nap on my coffee break.")

Other form: Meticulously *(adv)*

Sentence: Brian was fairly neat and careful about most things, but when it came to his stamp collection, he was absolutely *meticulous*.

FEATHERS

MINUTE (my-NOOT) *adj* — **very small in size**

Sounds like: my newt

Think of: A newt, which is a small salamander. A young boy is holding out his hand and saying to his older sister, "This is my newt." The sister, looking at the tiny spot on his hand, thinks he said "This is minute."

Other form: Minuteness *(noun)*

Connect with: Minutiae, which means minor details.

Sentence: A deer tick is *minute*, but it can cause big problems.

MISCONSTRUE (miss-kun-STROO) *verb* — **misunderstand; interpret incorrectly**

Sounds like: Miss Kahn's Two

Picture: Woman on the telephone at a restaurant called Miss Kahn's Two. She's speaking to a friend who thought they were supposed to meet at Miss Kahn's on the other side of town. Here's how they each misconstrued what the other was saying:

Woman 1: "I'm going out for dinner tonight."
Woman 2: "So am I. Where are you going?"
Woman 1: "I'm going to Miss Kahn's."
Woman 2: "Really? I'm going to Miss Kahn's, too!"
Woman 1: "Oh, okay. I'll see you there!"

Sentence: It's easy to *misconstrue* someone's meaning in an email, so be careful.

MITIGATE (MITT-uh-gate) *verb* — **make less severe; mollify**

Sounds like: middle gate

Picture: Return to the scene of the man cursing the gate (see CASTIGATE), but now the middle gate has calmed and soothed the angry man, to the relief of the first gate.

Sentence: Her soft tone had a *mitigating* effect, and the argument ended.

MOLLIFY (MOLL-ih-fie) *verb* — **lessen anger; soothe; placate**

Sounds like: Molly Fly

Picture: Molly Fly follows the Village Fly around; she soothes the feelings of the people he has upset (see VILIFY).

Sentence: Police try to *mollify* a hostage-taker to avoid violence.

MONOLOGUE (MONN-oh-log) *noun* — **a long, uninterrupted speech**

Sounds like: man on a log

Picture: A man standing on a log in the woods. His audience is a group of rabbits, foxes, mice, deer, raccoons, and birds, and they all look very tired from listening to his endless monologue: "...And so, my friends, let me remind you once again that we must be careful not to miss the forest for the trees..."

Sentence: After I ask how he is, I get comfortable and try to wait out his long *monologue*.

MOROSE (mawr-OSE) *adj* — **depressed**

Sounds like: more oats

Picture: Depressed horse at a bar. The bartender asks, "More oats, pal?"

Other forms: Moroseness *(noun)*; morosely *(adv)*

Sentence: I was already *morose*, and four days of rain made it worse.

MUNDANE (mun-DAYNE) *adj* — **ordinary; earthly (not spiritual); practical; temporary**

Sounds like: Monday

Picture: A weekly meeting of ghosts, gathering to discuss important matters of eternal and supernatural significance. However, one of the ghosts is only concerned about what day of the week it is. "Monday. Monday? Is today Monday? Our meetings are supposed to be held on Mondays. Shouldn't we check the calendar?" Another responds, "Clarence, we don't need to worry about such mundane matters."

Sentence: Some scientific theorists have trouble with *mundane* things, such as using a washing machine.

MYRIAD (MEER-ee-id) *adj* — **large number; many**

Sounds like: Mary had

Think of: The song, "Mary Had A Little Lamb." Now imagine that this lamb grew up and had little lambs of her own. And then *they* all had little lambs, and so on, so that in a few years, Mary had thousands of little lambs. (They all still followed her to school. Luckily, she went to a large university.)

Sentence: Most stores offer a *myriad* of choices.

NEFARIOUS (neh-FAIR-ee-uss) *adj* — **extremely evil**

Sounds like: no ferry is

Picture: A crazed, wicked modern-day pirate who attacks and plunders ferry boats filled with rush-hour commuters. "No ferry is safe from me," he proclaims.

Sentence: The gangster's *nefarious* ways shocked his mother, who thought he was a dentist.

NEGLIGENT (NEG-lih-jint) *adj* — **careless and possibly causing harm; neglectful**

Sounds like: negligee

Picture: Couple having breakfast. Husband is upset because wife accidentally baked her negligee into the blueberry pie and served it to their dinner guests last night.
He: "How could you be so careless?"
She: "It was a simple mistake. No harm done."
He: "No harm? Paul and Donna's little boy almost choked on that thing."
She: "Well, you'd better be careful when you eat your oatmeal. I'm missing a pair of stockings."

Other form: Negligence *(noun)*

Sentence: The driver was charged with *negligence* for leaving the scene of an accident.

NEOPHYTE
(NEE-oh-fite) *noun*
— **beginner**

Sounds like: neo-fighter

Picture: A nervous young boxer who is about to get into the ring for the first time.

Connect with: Any words that begin with "neo." They always refer to something that is new.

Sentence: Val was a *neophyte*, but learned quickly.

NOSTALGIC (nuh-STAL-jik) *adj*
— **wishing for a return to the way things used to be; longing for the past; homesick**

Sounds like: nose tell cheek

Picture: A face with stylish eyeglasses perched on the nose. The nose looks over to one cheek and says, "I miss the *old* glasses."

Other form: Nostalgia *(noun)*

Sentence: Seeing the pictures of her parents made Jane *nostalgic*.

NOCTURNAL (nok-TERN-il) *adj*
— **active at night**

Sounds like: knock, turn, Al

Picture: The local chapter of the "Midnight Club," a group of people who only go out late at night. Al is a new member and doesn't know how to get into the club's secret building. A whispering voice from the intercom system tries to help him: "Give the official Midnight Club knock on the door, then turn the knob. Got it? Knock, turn, Al!"

Other form: Nocturnally *(adv)*

Opposite: Diurnal *(adj)*

Sentence: Bats are *nocturnal*, so we rarely see them in daylight.

NOVELTY (NAH-vul-tee) *noun*
— **something new or unusual**

Sounds like: novel tea

Picture: A teacup with a novel as a teabag. Or, novels pouring out of a teapot's spout.

Other form: novel *(adj)*

Sentence: The microwave oven is no longer a *novelty*.

NUANCE (NOO-onts) *noun*
— **slight degree; shade of difference**

Sounds like: new ants

Picture: A "new ant" lot. The "vehicles" are ants, the salesman and customer are anteaters. Salesman explains the subtle ways in which this year's model differs from last year's.

Sentence: The *nuances* of opera aren't obvious to most of us.

NULLIFY (NUL-ih-fy) *verb* — **remove or cancel all value or force; negate**

Looks like: null if Y ("null" means "having no value")

Picture: Nellie has the airplane ticket in her hand as she speaks to an airline representative. He tells her that the ticket is null and void if the letter Y appears at the top. She looks, and sure enough, there's a Y. The ticket's value has been nullified.

Other forms: Nullification *(noun);* null *(adj)*

Sentence: The touchdown was *nullified* because the team had too many players on the field.

NURTURE (NER-cher) *verb* — **provide care and support; nourish; train or educate**

Sounds like: nurse chair

Picture: The maternity ward of a hospital. In one corner of the nursery is the Nurse Chair. In this large rocker, the nurse sits to feed and talk to the infants, giving them love and nourishment. Here is also where the new mothers come to learn from this experienced nurturer about caring for their babies.

Other forms: Nurturer, nurturance *(nouns)*

Sentence: A beautiful garden needs to be *nurtured* with water, fertilizer, and sunshine.

The following nine words begin with the letters "ob". Because "ob" sounds like "Hobb," the pictures for all of the words will involve Mr. Hobb.

OBDURATE (OB-der-it) *adj* — **stubborn; unyielding**

Sounds like: Hobb door 8

Picture: Hobb and his wife are looking for a friend's apartment. When Hobb knocks on door #8, a strange man answers. "I'm sorry," says Hobb's wife. "We must have the wrong apartment." But when the man closes the door, Hobb knocks on it again, insisting that it's where his friend lives. No matter how many times his wife and the man at the door assure him that it's the wrong apartment, Hobb refuses to listen and keeps going back to it.

Other forms: Obdurateness *(noun);* obdurately *(adv)*

Sentence: He was *obdurate* about cleanliness and bathed twice a day.

MR. HOBB, WILL YOU PLEASE CLOSE THE JURY GATE?! THIS IS THE THIRD TIME I'VE HAD TO ASK!

OBJURGATE (OBB-jur-gate) *verb* — **scold; castigate**

Looks like: Hobb jury gate

Picture: Hobb is on jury duty. He has just entered the enclosed area of the courtroom where the jury sits, but he's forgotten to close the gate. The judge scolds him: "Mr. Hobb, will you please close the jury gate! This is the third time I've had to remind you! How are you going to remember the details of this trial if you can't remember a simple thing like closing the gate?"

Other form: Objurgation *(noun)*

Sentence: The radio talk show host lost all patience and thoroughly *objurgated* the rude caller.

OBLITERATE (uh-BLIT-er-ate) *verb* — **remove or destroy completely; erase**

Looks like: Hobb litter ate

Picture: Hobb has just dropped some candy wrappers on the ground. When he rounds the corner he sees a police officer walking toward him. Hobb is afraid he'll get a ticket for littering, so he runs back around the corner and eats the wrappers! By the time the police officer arrives, the litter has been obliterated.

Other form: Obliteration *(noun)*

Sentence: The fire *obliterated* the building and its contents.

OBSCURE (obb-SKYOOR) *adj* — **hazy; unfamiliar; difficult to understand**

Sounds like: Hobb's cure

Picture: Patient coming out of Dr. Hobb's office. The patient's wife questions him about the visit:

Wife: What did Dr. Hobb say?
Patient: I'm not sure.
Wife: Well, did he say it was curable?
Patient: I think so, but maybe not. He was pretty vague.
Wife: What's that prescription for?
Patient: I have no idea. He told me, but I didn't understand.
Wife: Is this Hobb's Cure? Send your patient home in a fog?
Patient: It might be. How would I tell?

Other forms: Obscurely *(adv)*; obscurity *(noun)*

Sentence: Most people who are famous in their day eventually fade into *obscurity*.

OBSEQUIOUS (ob-SEEK-wee-us) *adj* — **behaving like a meek, spineless servant; subservient; sycophantic**

Sounds like: Hobb's sequins

Picture: Hobb's brother and his wife are visiting for a few days. One night, Hobb walks into the living room and finds his brother, in his wife's sequin dress, standing on a chair. Seeing the surprised expression on Hobb's face, the brother explains: "She told me to put it on so she can see how it looks from a distance. I'd do anything for my wife, and this is such a little favor. Tomorrow afternoon I'm going to wear it to our favorite restaurant so she can see how it looks in the light there. She wants me to."

Other forms: Obsequiousness *(noun)*; obsequiously *(adv)*

Sentence: A dictator will often surround himself with a large, *obsequious* staff.

OBSOLETE (obb-so-LEET) *adj* — **no longer usable; outdated**

Sounds like: Hobb so late

Picture: Hobb riding in a horse & buggy, arriving for an important meeting. His co-workers are annoyed at his lateness, and wonder why he's driving such an obsolete vehicle.

Other form: Obsolescence *(noun)*

Sentence: Manual typewriters would be considered *obsolete* in most modern offices.

75

OBSTINATE (OBB-stin-ett) *adj* — **stubborn; refusing to be persuaded**

Sounds like: Hobbs ten-eight

Picture: Hobb playing basketball with some of his friends. Hobb insists the score is ten-eight, even when assured by his opponents and his own teammates that the score is twelve-six. "Look," says Hobb, "I don't care that you all think it's twelve-six, or that we have spectators who agree with you, or that we have the game on videotape and that it shows the score to be twelve-six. I still say the score is ten-eight. Why should I change my mind?"

Other forms: Obstinacy *(noun);* obstinately *(adv)*

Sentence: Always *obstinate*, Sue insisted on going to the movies, even though she had the flu.

OBTUSE (obb-TOOSE) *adj* — **dull; blunt; unintelligent; lacking sharpness**

Sounds like: Hobb two's

Picture: Hobb as a young boy standing at the blackboard, where he has written "2 + 2 = 97."

Other forms: Obtuseness *(noun);* obtusely *(adv)*

Sentence: His *obtuse* argument convinced no one.

OBVIATE (OBB-vee-ate) *verb* — **eliminate the need for something; make unnecessary**

Sounds like: Hobb V-8

Picture: Hobb driving a very large, brand new car (with a V-8 engine) past his old horse & buggy (see OBSOLETE). Hobb tells the horse that he doesn't need him anymore.

Other form: Obviation *(noun)*

Sentence: Credit and debit cards have almost *obviated* the need for cash.

OMINOUS (OMM-in-uss) *adj* — **a sign of something unpleasant that's about to happen; inauspicious**

Sounds like: "Oh, my noose!"

Picture: A condemned man looking at the noose that will soon be placed around his neck. Growing extremely nervous, he says, "Oh, my noose!"

Other form: Omen *(noun);* ominously *(adv)*

Sentence: Centuries ago, people saw comets, eclipses, and other astronomical events as *ominous* signs of future trouble.

ONEROUS (OWN-er-uss) adj
— **burdensome; oppressive**

Sounds like: owner Russ

Picture: A man named Russ is scolding a teenager he's hired to wash and wax his expensive car: "Come on!" he yells. "Put some effort into it. Make that radio antenna shine!" ("Wow," thinks the exhausted young man. "This owner, Russ, is really creating a burden for me.")

Other forms: Onerousness *(noun)*; onerously *(adv)*

Sentence: Once an idealistic nurse, Pat now viewed the profession as an *onerous* way to make a living.

OPAQUE (oh-PAKE) adj — **too dark or thick for light to pass through**

Sounds like: oh cake

Picture: Right after the wedding reception, the newlyweds run to their car to leave for their honeymoon. They're surprised to find no "Just Married" sign on the back or bells hanging from the mirrors. But when they get into the car they notice the entire windshield has been covered by a thick, white substance, which they obviously can't see through. When they look more closely they say, "Oh, cake!"

Other form: Opacity *(noun)*

Sentence: The stain was *opaque* and hid the grain of the wood.

OPPORTUNIST (opper-TOON-ist) noun — **someone who takes advantage of the situation**

Sounds like: opera tunist (the man who tunes the instruments at the opera)

Picture: The lead singer faints and the opera tunist runs in to help: "I can sing! I'll take his place!"

Other form: Opportunistic *(adj)*

Sentence: An *opportunistic* lawsuit attorney, Tom enjoyed witnessing traffic accidents.

OPTIMIST (OPP-tih-mist) noun — **someone who always believes things will turn out okay**

Looks like: a combination of "optometrist" and "mist"

Picture: An optometrist (eye specialist) leading his family on a hike up the side of a mountain. The mist is heavy and they can't see anything, but he insists they'll make it: "I've developed these special glasses that help you see through mist. If we all put them on, I know we'll get to the top in a few minutes. And you know what else? I think there'll be a picnic lunch waiting for us up there. And soft chairs to sit on..."

Other forms: Optimistic *(adj)*; optimistically *(adv)*

Opposite: Pessimist *(noun)*

Sentence: You have to be an *optimist* if you're going to invest your money in the stock market.

OPULENCE (OPP-yoo-lence) noun — **luxury; wealth; riches**

Looks like: opal fence (opal is a precious gem)

Picture: We were visiting cousins in a wealthy part of the state. My brother and I wandered off and walked toward the lake, where we came upon a magnificent house in the woods. We saw six Rolls Royces parked in the long, circular driveway. The shrubs were sculpted to look like dollar signs. But the most amazing sight of all was the fence. It ran around the entire property and was made completely of opal. It glistened and shone in the afternoon sun, the brightest, most luxurious thing we had ever seen.

Other forms: Opulent *(adj)*; opulently *(adv)*

Sentence: To many people from other nations, an average American home would seem *opulent*.

PACIFIST (PASS-uh-fist) *noun* — **person who refuses to fight**

Sounds like: pass a fist

Picture: Bully standing with his fist raised, threatening a smaller man. But the smaller guy refuses to fight and walks past the fist.

Other form: Pacify *(verb)*   Connect with: Pacific, pacifier, peaceful

Sentence: It was hard for Einstein, a *pacifist*, to support the war against Germany.

PALTRY (PAWL-tree) *adj* — **worthless; insignificant, petty**

Sounds like: poultry

Remember Kate and the eggs truck? (See EXTRICATE.) Okay, so the driver goes to the back of the truck and rescues Kate. But she's very angry, and when he tries to explain that the crazed chicken made him drive off so wildly, Kate says, "Well, that's a poultry excuse!" (She means 'paltry,' or worthless, but the driver is too scared to correct her.)

Other form: Paltriness *(noun)*   Sentence: Bill could barely survive on his *paltry* wages.

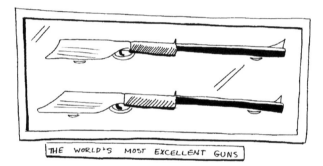

THE WORLD'S MOST EXCELLENT GUNS

PARAGON (PAHR-a-gon) *noun* — **model of excellence; the best**

Sounds like: pair of guns

Picture: The world's most perfect guns.

Sentence: Fred Astaire was a *paragon* of dance.

PARITY (PAHR-ih-tee) *noun* — **equality or equivalence; balance among a group of rivals**

Looks like: party

Picture: A boy is having a birthday party at his house. On the same day, the girl next door is having *her* birthday party. Holding a pair of binoculars, the boy watches everything that happens at the other party, then runs to his mother and demands equality. "Her cake is chocolate with pink frosting. That's what I want. And a clown just showed up. Where's my clown? She has bigger balloons..."

Note: Don't confuse with "parody," which refers to an imitation that is meant to poke fun at the subject.

Sentence: There is *parity* in a sports league when no one team dominates every year.

PARSIMONY (par-SIMM-uh-nee) *noun* — **stinginess; excessive frugality**

Looks like: parsley money

Picture: A woman at a fruit and vegetable stand, haggling with the owner about the price of parsley: "Look, I budget forty-nine cents a month for parsley, and that's all I'm going to pay for it."

Other form: Parsimonious *(adj)*

Sentence: His *parsimony* made him an unpopular school board treasurer.

PARTISAN (PAR-tih-zin) *adj*
— **blindly devoted to a cause or organization**

Sounds like: party sun

Picture: A member of an unknown country's military. He's been assigned to a secret mission by the ruling *party*: they want to put him in a rocket ship and send him to the *sun*. As any member of his party would be, he is honored. "Of course I will do it," he says. "It is a privilege. It is what every faithful party member waits for all his life. This will be my moment in the sun."

Other forms: Partisan, partisanship *(nouns)*

Sentence: It's easy for members of a club or political group to see things from a *partisan* perspective.

PECUNIARY (peh-KYOON-ee-er-ee) *adj*
— **having to do with money; financial**

Sounds like: petuniary, or petunias

Picture: Petunias with dollar bills for flowers.

Sentence: A corporate leader must often consider the *pecuniary* aspect of decisions.

PAUCITY (PAW-sih-tee) *noun*
— **too few; scarcity**

Sounds like: poor city

Picture: A poor city consisting entirely of slums. There is a scarcity of everything in this city: the citizens lack the things they need.

Sentence: In many of the poorer nations of Africa, there is a dangerous *paucity* of food and medicine.

I CAN'T HELP IT... I HAVE A PENCHANT FOR THEM.

PENCHANT (PENCH-ent) *noun*
— **a strong liking; attraction**

Sounds like: pendant

Picture: A woman with many pendants around her neck. She obviously has a strong liking for them.

Sentence: A *penchant* for antique cars can be an expensive trait.

PENURY (PEN-yer-ee) *noun* — **extreme poverty; destitution**

Sounds like: pen Yuri

Picture: The same guy named Yuri who used to lend money at extremely high interest rates (see USURY). His customers finally caught on to Yuri, and now he's on the street, completely penniless, trying to earn food money by selling old pens. His new slogan: "Please buy from Pen Yuri. I'm broke."

Other forms: Penurious *(adj)*; penuriously *(adv)*

Sentence: Banks are reluctant to lend money to people who need it most -- those living in *penury*.

PERFUNCTORY (per-FUNK-ter-ee) *adj* — **without enthusiasm or thoroughness; routine**

Looks like: perfume factory

Picture: The woman responsible for inspecting a perfume factory has just completed her tour in a little under three minutes. Her assistant, a young man in training, is amazed at how short their inspection was: "We hardly looked at anything in there. What kind of inspection is this?" Her response: "A perfunctory one. Look, why should I push myself? I've been through here a hundred times before. I never find anything, I write them a positive report, and I always come out smelling like a rose!"

Sentence: He'd been teaching the course for so long, it had become a *perfunctory* exercise.

PERNICIOUS (per-NISH-uss) *adj* — **destructive**

Sounds like: burn his shoes

Picture: A man in a prison cell. The man's cellmate is destructive, and one day, when he comes back to the cell he finds that his shoes have been burned up.

Other forms: Perniciousness *(noun);* perniciously *(adv)*

Sentence: He was a *pernicious* boy who broke all his toys.

PERSPICACITY (per-spih-KASS-it-ee) *noun* — **mental sharpness; keen insight; shrewdness**

Sounds like: perspire Cassidy

Picture: Cassidy's been brought down to police headquarters for questioning. There doesn't seem to be any evidence at all against him, but as the detective asks his probing questions, he makes a shrewd observation: "You say you weren't there, but I notice you're starting to perspire, Cassidy. Is it possible you know more about this crime than you're admitting?"

Other forms: Perspicacious *(adj);* perspicaciously *(adv)*

Sentence: Carly was normally *perspicacious*, but the high altitude was clouding her mind.

PERUSE (puh-ROOZ) *verb* — **read carefully; study in detail**

Sounds like: Peru's

Picture: A man carefully reading a giant map of Peru.   Other form: Perusal *(noun)*

Sentence: If you thought you were inheriting a fortune, you would want to *peruse* the will thoroughly.

PERVADE (per-VADE) *verb* — **to spread to every part**

Sounds like: parade

Picture: It had been raining all morning, but just as the parade began, the clouds moved away and the sun appeared. Instantly, a feeling of joy pervaded the crowd (marchers and spectators alike.)

Other forms: Pervasiveness, pervasion *(nouns);* pervasive *(adj)*; pervasively *(adv)*

Sentence: The fire was *pervasive* and smoke had spread to every apartment.

PETULANCE (PETCH-oo-lence) *noun* — **grouchiness**

Sounds like: pet chew Lance

Picture: Lance has a dog who likes to chew on one of those fake rawhide bones. The dog chews all day and even in his sleep, and has been doing this for years. But today Lance is in a bad mood. He's not sure why, but he's cranky, and his pet is just chewing and chewing on that bone and it's getting on his nerves. Finally, Lance can't take it anymore: "Would you stop chewing on that stupid bone? All day and all night for eight years I've been listening to you chomp on that thing. I've been patient, extremely patient, I think, but I have to tell you that it's driving me absolutely crazy!"

Other forms: Petulant *(adj)*; petulantly *(adv)*

Sentence: He felt justified in his *petulance*, but friends began to avoid him.

PHLEGMATIC (fleg-MAT-ick) *adj*
— **calm; unemotional**

Sounds like: flag medic

Picture: A medic (military doctor) holding a flag. Fireworks light up the sky behind them, but both the medic and flag remain limp.

Sentence: Anne was *phlegmatic*, almost strangely serene, during the holdup.

PIOUS (PIE-us) *adj*
— **exhibiting religious devotion**

Sounds like: pies

Picture: Pies praying. Or someone praying to a pie.

Other forms: Piety *(noun)*; piously *(adv)*

Sentence: He never went to church or temple, but he was *pious* all the same.

PITHY (PITH-ee) *adj* — **to the point; concise**

Sounds like: pity

Picture: A TV news reporter stands at someone's front door. "Sir, you live next door to Mr. Jobe, whose house, as you know, was flattened by an asteroid around noon today. What you may not know is that Mr. Jobe was served with divorce papers this morning while he was at court filing for personal bankruptcy. Shorty afterward, his car was stolen while he was having emergency root canal work done, and so he has been unable to see the charred shell of his house. Would you tell our audience what you think of the kind of day Mr. Jobe has been having?" The man says simply, "Pity."

Other forms: Pith, pithiness *(nouns)*   Sentence: An effective note is clear and *pithy*.

PLACATE (PLAY-kate) *verb* — **to appease; pacify; mollify**

Sounds like: play Kate

Picture: Three girls are playing hopscotch on the sidewalk. Kate, who is younger than the others, is sitting on a nearby bench, obviously upset that she's been excluded from the game. Finally, in an effort to pacify her, one of the girls says, "It's okay, you can play, Kate." When she hears the invitation, Kate's face lights up and she happily joins the others.

Other form: Placatory *(adj)*   Sentence: She was skillful at *placating* unhappy customers.

PLATITUDE (PLAT-ih-tood) *noun* — **dull, trite statement**

Sounds like: plate a tooth

Picture: A dental office. The patient is having one of his teeth plated. (Whatever that means. I don't know, maybe it doesn't mean anything. I'm not a dentist. Anyway, it doesn't matter, just pretend you know what plating is.) So he's in the chair and he has about eighteen different clamps in and around his mouth, his gums are filled with cotton balls, the little suction thing is stuck to his tongue, and he tastes blood. The dentist, meanwhile, is trying to be entertaining. But all he can come up with is one stupid, boring remark after another, like "Isn't this an experience you can sink your *teeth* into?" "I hope this doesn't take too much of a *bite* out of your bank account!" "Just relax. You won't feel any pain, just a little pressure..."

Sentence: Voters were hoping for a forceful and targeted speech, but they got the usual *platitudes*.

PLAUSIBLE (PLAWS-ih-bull) *adj* — **believable, but not completely**

Sounds like: Claus or Bill

Picture: Two little girls studying the Santa Claus who has appeared at their door. They want to believe it's really Santa Claus, and they're 95% sure it is, but there's just something about his voice that tells them it might be their neighbor, Bill. "It definitely *could* be the real Santa Claus," says one. "Well, I say we give him the benefit of the doubt," says the other. "That 'Ho Ho Ho' sounded plausible to me."

Other forms: Plausibility *(noun);* plausibly *(adv)*

Sentence: Most of the movie seemed *plausible*, but that ending was ridiculous.

POMPOUS (POMP-us) *adj* — **filled with self-importance; arrogant; obnoxiously proud**

Sounds like: pom-poms

Picture: The new head cheerleader at the high school has just been chosen and she has decided to appear before an assembly of the entire school to tell everyone how much she deserves the honor and how lucky they are to have her. "And now," she says, waving her pom-poms over her head, "how about a big cheer for me?"

Other forms: Pomposity *(noun);* pompously *(adv)*

Sentence: The new manager seemed like a *pompous* jerk who wasn't interested in anyone else's ideas.

PONDEROUS (PONN-der-uss) *adj* — **slow; weighty; labored**

Sounds like: pond of rust

Picture: Creatures made of metal wading through a pond. As they begin to rust, their movements become slower and more difficult.

Other form: Ponderously *(adv)*

Sentence: The music was heavy and *ponderous*, and I fell alseep.

PORTENT (POR-tent) *noun*
— **warning sign; omen; indication**

Sounds like: poor tent

Picture: A wife, husband, son, and daughter on their first camping trip. The children are watching their parents try to pitch the tent. When the tent is finally up, it is small, shaky, and has several holes in it. The daughter says to her brother, "I have a feeling that poor tent is a sign of things to come this weekend."

Other forms: Portend *(verb)*; portentious *(adj)*

Sentence: The full moon was a *portent* that the creature would soon appear.

POTENT (PO-tent) *adj* — **powerful**

Looks like: patent

Picture: Two boys in their classroom, the teacher unconscious on the floor. One boy says to the other, "Hey, we should patent that spitball. It's potent!"

Other form: Potency *(noun)*

Connect with: Potentate, potential

Sentence: The team has a *potent* offense.

PRECLUDE (pre-KLOOD) *verb*
— **prevent; make impossible**

Sounds like: pre-glued

Picture: Young boy proudly showing his father a large stack of envelopes; there is a bottle of glue on the desk. "Hey, Dad, these envelopes of yours were supposed to be pre-glued but I don't think they were. So I decided to save you a lot of work by glueing them closed. Pretty smart, huh?" (Father thinks: "Well, I guess this precludes me from mailing anything in those envelopes.")

Other forms: Preclusion *(noun)*; preclusive *(adj)*

Sentence: The still-flooded streets *precluded* the parade from going on as scheduled.

PRECARIOUS (pree-KAIR-ee-yuss) *adj*
— **risky; uncertain**

Sounds like: please carry us

Picture: Two children following their father on a hike along the edge of a cliff. "Dad," cries one of them, "We're afraid we might fall. Please carry us."

Other forms: Precariously *(adv)*; precariousness *(noun)*

Sentence: Mountain climbers often find themselves in *precarious*, potentially deadly, situations.

PRECOCIOUS (pre-KO-shuss) *adj*
— **mature at a young age**

Sounds like: pre-coat shoes

Picture: A young boy dressed in a business suit. His mother is admiring his stylish shoes. "Those are beautiful shoes, dear. Just don't forget to wear your coat." The boy's response: "Please don't talk to me as though I were a child, Mother. I am, after all, nearly eight years old."

Other forms: Precociously *(adv)*; precocity *(noun)*

Sentence: Child actors are often *precocious*, able to seem more grown-up than they are.

PREDECESSOR (PRED-ih-sess-or) *noun* — **an earlier occupant of a job, office, or position**

Sounds like: pretty scissor

Picture: Two servants are talking in the mansion where they work. The man is admiring the woman's scissors, which are sterling silver and have precious stones set into the handles around the finger holes. "What pretty scissors!" he says. "Yes," she responds, "they were given to me by my predecessor. She worked here as the family's coupon clipper for nearly thirty years!"

Sentence: She completely redecorated the office, removing all evidence of her *predecessor*.

PREDILECTION (pred-ih-LEK-shun) *noun* — **a preference for something**

Sounds like: bread election

Picture: The judge at a bread baking contest. The different loaves are displayed on a table, but the judge is looking away, eyes closed. She knew right from the beginning which bread she would choose.

Sentence: Marty's *predilection* for brownies meant he was constantly battling his weight.

PRETENTIOUS (pre-TENCH-us) *adj* — **showy; making ridiculous claims; excessively ambitious**

Sounds like: pretend shoes

Picture: A man showing his new shoes to his family. He is proud of everything he does, to the point of being unrealistic. But regarding these shoes, he seems to be even more out of touch with reality than usual. He calls them his "pretend shoes," and he says that while wearing them, he'll be able to fly.

Other forms: Pretension *(nouns)*; pretentiously *(adv)*

Sentence: The house was *pretentious*, clearly designed and decorated to make visitors feel inferior.

PREVALENT (PREV-uh-lent) *adj* — **widely-accepted; common; prevailing**

Sounds like: provolone (a type of cheese)

Picture: You're visiting a small village in Italy. Almost immediately you notice that everywhere you go in this village, you see provolone cheese. In the shops, people are buying it; in the restaurants, people are eating it; in the streets, people are holding it. You see provolone cheese on TV and in magazines. Even the mayor's name is Dom Provolone. It is, in this small Italian town, a very common cheese.

Other forms: Prevalence *(noun)*

Sentence: The English language is *prevalent* throughout the world.

PRIMORDIAL (pry-MOR-dee-al) *adj* — **formed long ago; primitive**

Sounds like: pry Morty, Al

Picture: Two archeologists have been digging in the hard soil of Turkey and have discovered the skeleton of a primitive man. As they take turns digging out "Morty," as they have nicknamed the skeleton, the archeologists cheer each other on. When Al takes his turn, his partner encourages him to pry the skeleton out from beneath a stone: "Pry him out. Pry Morty, Al. But be careful, he's very old."

84   Sentence: What amazing creatures must have lived in the *primordial* forests?

PRODIGAL (PROD-ih-gull) *adj*
— wasteful, especially of money; extravagant

Sounds like: proud of gulls

Picture: Person who has spent his entire inheritance to buy a flock of seagulls. He's very proud of his purchase, not realizing that he's squandered his fortune.

Note: Don't confuse with "prodigy," a highly-talented child.

Sentence: Sal earned enough, but his *prodigal* nature caused him to live beyond his means.

PRODIGIOUS (pro-DIJ-uss) *adj* — **very large**

Sounds like: pro dishes

Picture: Large dishes. Prodigious is often used to describe a person's enormous appetite, so you might imagine someone eating a large amount of food from very large dishes.

Other forms: Prodigiousness *(noun);* prodigiously *(adv)*

Sentence: After a twenty-year career, her accomplishments were *prodigious*.

PROFOUND (pro-FOWND) *adj* — **filled with wisdom and insight; beyond the superficial; deep**

Looks like: Prof. Found

Picture: A philosophy professor from the local college had been missing for a week, but he's been discovered alive and well, trapped at the bottom of an abandoned mine shaft. The headline in today's newspaper: "PROF FOUND!" Upon first seeing his rescuers, the professor looks up and says, "I am a symbol of mankind, fallen from the heights of power and wisdom to the depths of despair and destitution, until you, the gods of Goodness and Health, arrived to bring me the gifts of freedom and rebirth." Looking down from the top of the mine shaft, one rescuer says to the other: "Wow, that's deep!"

Other forms: Profundity *(noun);* profoundly *(adv)* Don't confuse with "profane," which means "vulgar" or "disrespectful of sacred things" (profanity).

Sentence: Tina came through the ordeal with a new and *profound* understanding of life.

PROFUSE (pro-FYOOS) *adj* — **in large amounts or quantities**

Looks like: Prof. Fuse

Picture: A physics instructor named Prof. Fuse has invited you into his office. As you enter, you notice that the room is overflowing with fuses of all kinds — car fuses, boat fuses, house fuses. Everywhere you look — on the shelves, under the desk, in the light fixtures — are hundreds of fuses. "Prof. Fuse," you say, "what a profusion of fuses!" (It's a weird thing to say, but it fits.)

Other forms: Profuseness, profusion *(noun);* profusely *(adv)*

Sentence: The *profusion* of food on the cruise was overwhelming, and we stuffed ourselves.

PROTRACT (pro-TRAKT) *verb* — **extend in time or space**

Sounds like: pro track

Picture: Young women running on a track. Eventually they notice that a crew of workmen is digging up the track in order to make it bigger. The men explain to the runners: "No more amateur stuff. This is going to be a pro track from now on, so we have to make it regulation size for professional races."

Other forms: Protraction *(noun);* protractive *(adj)*

Sentence: The meeting was *protracted*, and she had to cancel her plans for the evening.

PROVOKE (pruh-VOKE) *verb* — **to anger; to stir up or arouse**

Sounds like: prove oak

Picture: Two women out in the forest. One points out a tree and says it's an oak. The other disagrees; she thinks it's some other kind of tree. As they walk, the first woman pulls "The Tree Handbook" out of her coat pocket, opens up to the section on oaks, and proves to her friend that the tree in question is indeed an oak. Not satisfied with being right, she then resorts to mocking and insulting her companion with comments such as: "What kind of tree did you *think* it was? I mean, any fool could see that was an oak from a mile away! You must be the dumbest living thing in this forest! Let me ask you this, did you know it was a tree?" The victim of this provocation grows angrier and angrier, until she cannot listen any more. She bends down, picks up a small oak log, and whacks her friend over the head with it.

Other forms: Provocative *(adj)*; provokingly *(adv);* provocation *(noun)*

Sentence: People involved in a long-running feud often don't even know what *provoked* it.

PROXIMITY (proks-IM-ih-tee) *noun* — **nearness; closeness**

Looks like: a combination of "approximate" and "vicinity." Something in the approximate vicinity is nearby.

Other forms: Proximate *(adj)*; proximately *(adv)*

Sentence: Joe sold his car because his house was in such *proximity* to everything.

PUERILE (PYUR-ill) or (PYUR-ile) *adj* — **childish**

"Puerile" looks like a combination of "purely" and "juvenile." Juvenile means childish, so think of someone who's purely juvenile.

Other form: Puerility *(noun)*

Sentence: If you want to see *puerile* behavior, go to a Little League game -- and watch the parents.

PRUDENT (PROO-dent) *adj* — **wise; shrewd; cautious**

Sounds like: prune dent

Picture: Two gangs are on opposite sides of the street. They're having their monthly prune war, in which they continue to throw prunes at each other until one side gives up. Your car is parked in the street, directly in the line of fire. It's a new car, without a scratch, and you wish to keep it that way. So, to avoid prune dents and other such blemishes, you prudently run to the car and drive it to safety.

Other forms: Prudently *(adv);* prudence *(noun);* prudential *(adj)*

Sentence: Sometimes the most *prudent* thing to say is nothing at all.

QUALIFY (KWAL-ih-fye) *verb* — **to limit the meaning of a previous statement; to modify**

Sounds like: Wally Fly.   Sounds exactly like: qualify (as in, to be suitable for a position)
Let's combine the two.

Picture: Wally Fly is a fly who screens applicants wishing to work directly for the queen. When she asks him if a certain candidate is qualified for the job, he replies, "Yes, Your Highness, I would be willing to bet my life that he is qualified... Well, maybe not my life, but I'd risk my job to say he's the right one. I take that back. I don't mean that if he doesn't work out that you should fire me. I'm just saying that he's the best applicant we've had. Well, so far, anyway. I doubt very much that we'll get a better one. But then again, a better one could come along. Who knows, really...?"

Other forms: Qualifier *(noun);* qualified *(adj)*

Sentence: He *qualified* his original promise so many times, I couldn't remember what the promise was.

QUANDARY (KWON-dree) *noun* — **a state of confusion or doubt; dilemma**

Sounds like: coin tree

Picture: An apple tree filled with ripe apples. The tree has what appears to be a coin slot in the middle of its trunk. A woman approaches and reads a sign next to the tree: "Apples 25 cents. Please deposit correct change in slot." The woman seems to be confused and unsure what to do. She's in a quandary.

Sentence: The need to make quick medical decisions for someone else can send anyone into a *quandary.*

QUARANTINE (KWAR-en-teen) *noun* — **forced isolation to prevent the spread of disease**

Sounds like: car and teen

Picture: Sick teenager locked inside a car. "I can't come out for forty days?" he asks. "But really, it's just allergies!"

Other form: Quarantine *(verb);* quarantined *(adj)*

Sentence: The first astronauts to return from the Moon were *quarantined* until they could be examined.

QUELL (KWELL) *verb* — **to calm; pacify**

Looks like: a combination of 'queen' and 'quill'

Picture: A violent riot is taking place just outside the castle. The queen comes to a window, waves a quill (feather) over the crowd, and everyone immediately calms down and goes peacefully home.

Sentence: Her fears were *quelled* as soon as she saw her friends approach the campsite.

QUERULOUS (KWER-uh-luss) *adj* — **constantly complaining**

Sounds like: squirrel louse

Picture: Squirrel loudly complaining about a louse that's biting his back. (Louse is the singular of lice.)

Note: Querulous is *not* related to the word "query," which means to question.

Sentence: His critical, *querulous* nature was hard to live with.

RAMPANT (RAMM-pent) *adj* — **unrestrained; widespread**

Looks like: ramp ant

Picture: Thousands of ants running up the ramp to the ark. Noah is saying, "Two! I said two!" (Looking on, one anteater says to the other: "And you were worried about the food on this cruise.")

Sentence: During the hot, dry summer, forest fires were *rampant*.

RATIFY (RAT-ih-fy) *verb* — **approve (by formal vote, for example); confirm**

Sounds like: rat to fly

Picture: The pilots' union has just ratified a new agreement with the airlines. As part of the agreement, rats will be allowed to fly commercial jets (but only if they meet the height requirement).

Other form: Ratification *(noun)*

Sentence: Congress *ratified* the new law by an overwhelming majority.

REBUFF (ree-BUFF) *verb* — **to ignore or reject strongly; snub**

Looks like: re-buff

Picture: A young woman is waxing and buffing her car for the third time that day. Without even looking away from the car, she says to a young man passing by, "No, Jerry, I can't go out with you tonight. I have to re-buff my car. Quite a few more times. Try me again, maybe in October."

Sentence: *Rebuffed* repeatedly, Marcia refused to give up and was finally hired.

REBUTTAL (re-BUTT-ul) *noun* — **denial or contradiction; argument; refutation**

Sounds like: re-butter

Picture: Husband and wife are both judges. One evening, at the dinner table with their two children, they get into a courtroom scene about whether the butter is too hard for the bread.

She: "This butter is just the right consistency. I submit that if you're careful about taking thin slices, Dear, it spreads quite easily on the bread."
He: "You say the butter is the right consistency, *Darling*. But isn't it true that while I wasn't looking, you secretly ran your knife under the hot water so that it would soften the butter when you used it?"
She: "I would like to call my first witness to the stand. Our daughter, Jennifer."
Jennifer to her brother: "I wish we could just eat dinner like everybody else."
Brother: "Yeah. And why do they have to wear those stupid robes every night?"

Other form: Rebut *(verb)*   Sentence: His *rebuttal* made her testimony seem implausible.

RECANT (re-CANT) *verb*
— **take back something you've said;
    withdraw a statement or belief**

Sounds like: recount

Picture: A candidate speaking to supporters
on the night of a close election: "My friends,
earlier this evening, I demanded a recount of
the votes. I am now recanting that request. I do
not want a recount, and am conceding defeat.
(See CONCEDE)

Sentence: Malcolm changed his mind and
recanted his original story about the robbery.

RECLUSE (REK-loose) *noun*
— **person who prefers to be alone all
    the time; someone withdrawn
    from the rest of society**

Sounds like: wreck clues

Picture: A woman walking backward, about to
enter her log cabin in the woods. As she walks,
she sweeps away her footprints in the snow.
"Have to wreck these clues," she says, "so no
one will find me. I don't want to see *anyone*."

Other forms: Reclusive *(adj);* reclusion *(noun)*

Sentence: After his wife died he lived alone, a
virtual *recluse*, for twenty years.

RECONDITE (REK-un-dite) *adj*
— **hidden; difficult to understand; profound**

Sounds like: reckon I

Picture: A young man has wandered into a
secret corner in the basement of the public
library, where he's found a large, dusty book
called, "The Mysteries of Life." After reading a
few pages in the book, he says, "I reckon I don't
understand what any of this means."

Other forms: Reconditeness *(noun);*
reconditely *(adv)*

Sentence: The strange, *recondite* message
scrawled on the wall bewildered everyone.

REDOLENT (REDD-uh-lint) *adj*
— **strongly scented; fragrant**

Sounds like: red doe lint

Picture: A doe (female deer) has red lint on her
back. The lint is giving off a very powerful
fragrance, which has attracted a male deer.
("You scent for me?" he asks.)

Other form: Redolence *(noun)*

Sentence: The spring air was *redolent* with cut
grass and lilacs.

REDUNDANT (re-DUN-dent) *adj*
— **more than what is necessary; in speech
    or writing, a repetition of words or ideas**

Sounds like: Red done that

Picture: Two children are given a list of
chores by their mother. As she reads off the
list, they respond to each item by saying,
"Red done that!" Red is their older brother,
and he has already done everything on the
list. Their mother, however, still wants them
to do each chore. "But, Mom!" plead the
children. "Isn't that redundant?" "Yes," she
responds. "It is redundant. It's also more than
what is necessary. And in speech or writing,
it's a repetition of words or ideas. Now go
do it anyway."

Other forms: Redundancy *(noun);*
redundantly *(adv)*

Sentence: It would be *redundant* to say
that the water was cold and frigid.

RELEGATE (RELL-uh-gate) *verb* — **reduce or demote to an inferior place or position; banish**

Sounds like: reel a gate

Picture: As head butler at the estate, he'd been in charge of a staff of thirty. But when the boss died and the young brat took over the house, he was demoted to the most meaningless and embarrassing job of all: he had to sit out on the lawn with a fishing pole. The fishing line was attached to the front gate, and when a visitor's car came up the driveway, he reeled in the gate until it opened.

Other form: Relegation *(noun)*

Sentence: After making one too many mistakes, Tim was *relegated* to a harmless position.

RELEVANCY (RELL-uh-vent-see) *noun* — **having a clear relationship to the matter at hand**

Sounds like: really fancy

Picture: A student named Germaine is answering a question about the planet Neptune, but he is bringing up things that have nothing (or very little) to do with the question: "Well, see, when they discovered the planet Neptune, the man who found it was living in this really fancy house in a really fancy town, and his wife had on this really fancy dress and they went out to celebrate at this really fancy restaurant..." The teacher finally interrupts: "Germaine, that's all very interesting but I don't think it's relevant."

Other forms: Relevant *(adj)*; relevance *(noun)*

Sentence: A newspaper headline should have a clear *relevancy* to the article that follows it.

REMORSE (ree-MORSE) *noun* — **a feeling of guilt; regret; self-reproach**

Looks exactly like: re-Morse (as in Morse Code)

Picture: A man sending a second message to his girlfriend by Morse Code. He taps out on the telegraph that he's sorry for what he said in his first message. The dots and dashes say simply, "FEELING GUILTY. VERY SORRY. PLEASE FORGIVE."

Other forms: Remorseful *(adj);* remorsefully *(adv)*

Sentence: After the guilty verdict was read, the defendant showed no *remorse* for what he'd done.

These "rep" words form the names of elected representatives.

REPRIMAND (REP-rih-mand) *verb*
— **scold; criticize**

Sounds like: Rep. Raymond

Picture: Representative Raymond has an unusual approach to campaigning. He walks around town scolding and criticizing the voters for their beliefs. (Read about his colleague — see REPROVE.)

Sentence: In addition to being fined, Jim was harshly *reprimanded* for failing to stop at the red light.

REPROVE (re-PROOV) *verb*
— **scold; criticize; disapprove of**

Sounds like: Rep. Prove

Picture: From the same city as Rep. Raymond, Rep. Prove takes the same approach to campaigning: he stops people on the street, asks for their opinion, tries to *prove* them wrong, them criticizes them.

Other forms: Reproval, reproof *(nouns)*

Sentence: Lynn was hurt by her father's *reproof.*

REPUDIATE (reh-PYOOD-ee-ate) *verb* — **disown; reject**

Sounds like: Rep. Rudy Yate

Picture: Representative Rudy Yate is running for re-election. He recently announced that he would disown, reject, and positively repudiate all those gifts he received from local businesses the last time he campaigned ("If I can still find 'em, of course.")

Other form: Repudiation *(noun)*

Sentence: Pam *repudiated* her membership and any connection with the organization.

THERE IS ONE RESERVED RESERVE.

RESERVE (ree-ZURV) *noun* — **the ability to control your emotions and actions; self-restraint**

Sounds exactly like: reserve (as in Army Reserve — a person in the Army on a part-time basis).

Picture: A private being screamed at by the sergeant. The other privates look on, amazed by their friend's ability to stay calm and unemotional as he endures his punishment.

Other form: Reserved *(adj)*

Sentence: He appeared to be *reserved*, but on the inside he was a tangle of emotions.

RESIGN (re-ZYNE) *verb* — **give in; acquiesce; relinquish**

Sounds exactly like: resign (as in, quit a job)

Picture: A Cabinet member is surrounded by the President, Vice President, all the other Cabinet members, and the president's staff. This particular Cabinet member is disliked by nearly everyone in the administration, as well as much of the general public. As he looks around the room at a sea of hostile faces he says, "All right, all right, I can't fight all of you. I guess I'll have to resign."

Other forms: Resigned *(adj)*; resignation *(noun)*; resignedly *(adv)*

Sentence: All of the roads were clogged with traffic, and Ellen *resigned* herself to being late.

RESOLVE (ree-ZOLVE) *noun* — **determination; strong will**

Looks like: re-solve (solve again)

Picture: A detective has just received word that a case he solved ten years ago has been re-opened because of new evidence. The detective spent many months on the case the first time, partly because the victim was a close friend of his. He's determined to solve the case again, no matter how long it takes. "My New Year's Resolution will be to re-solve this case," he says, "and put it to rest once and for all."

Other forms: Resolved, resolute *(adj)*; resolution *(noun)*; resolve *(verb)* Note: A New Year's Resolution is a promise that you are going to do something that requires a great deal of determination.

Sentence: Once Larry *resolved* to quit smoking, he kicked the habit and never looked back.

RETICENT (RETT-ih-sent) *adj* — **quiet; uncommunicative**

Sounds like: redder cent

Picture: A giant penny is being painted red. The penny sits quietly as the artist repeatedly asks, "Redder, Cent. Do you want to be redder? Cent? Huh? Penny for your thoughts. Hello, Cent..."

Other forms: Reticence *(noun)*; reticently *(adv)*

Sentence: He was normally a talkative boy, so his sudden *reticence* seemed to signal a problem.

REVERE (ree-VEER) *verb* — **greatly respect**

Sounds exactly like: Revere (Paul Revere's last name)

Picture: Young boy and girl dwarfed by large statue of Paul Revere. They are looking at the statue with great respect.

Other form: Reverence *(noun)*

Sentence: Winston Churchill was *revered* as a great statesman.

PAUL-REVERE

Now THERE'S SOMEONE YOU CAN LOOK UP TO.

ROTUND (roe-TUND) *adj* — **round**

Looks like: round, with a T in the middle

Picture: The word ROTUND in large letters. The "T" has dropped down to serve as a pedestal for the other letters, which spell the word ROUND.

Other form: Rotundity *(noun)*

Sentence: We could see the elephants' *rotund* silhouettes.

RUDIMENTARY (rood-ih-MEN-ter-ee) *adj* — **undeveloped; fundamental; elementary**

Looks like: Rudy elementary

Picture: Rudy's Elementary School, where the students learn only the simplest of concepts. In math, they never get past 2+2; in spelling, 'cat' is the most difficult word they study; in art, they get an 'A' if they can distinguish red from yellow.

Other form: Rudiment *(noun)*

Sentence: Most of the people were inadequately clothed and living in *rudimentary* houses.

SALUBRIOUS (suh-LOOB-ree-uss) *adj* — **promoting health**

Looks like: Sal's Libraries

Picture: A library owned by a man named Sal. The library is filled with books and magazines, but they're all about health. Library patron: "Excuse me, sir, do you have any books on disease, sickness, or death?" Sal: "Sorry, at Sal's Libraries we only have books on health." (See SALUTARY.)

Other form: Salubrity *(noun)*

Sentence: For some people, a day of sailing can have a most *salubrious* effect.

SALUTARY (SAL-yoo-terr-ee) *adj* — **promoting health, or having some beneficial effect**

Sounds like: Sal U. Terry

Picture: A traveling salesman in the 1800s. He's talking to a small crowd about "Sal U. Terry's Amazing Health & Vitality Elixir. It's guaranteed to make you feel better within one week, or you come and find me for a full refund. And if you need more information, just go down to one of Sal's Libraries and read all about this healthy concoction."

Connect with: Salubrious
Note: Don't confuse with "salutatory," which has to do with a welcome or greeting.

Sentence: The *salutary* qualities of garlic have been known for centuries.

SANCTION (SANK-shun) *verb* — **approve; give consent**

Sounds like: sank Shawn

Picture: You're rowing a boat out on the lake. Shawn, a man you've hated for eleven years, is rowing his boat on the other side of the lake. A friend suddenly shows up in the water right next to your boat and tells you that he just sank Shawn. The friend still holds the drill he used to bore a hole in the bottom of Shawn's boat. You pause for a second, then smile and say, "Good work. I normally don't like that kind of behavior, but if you tell me you sank Shawn, I have to approve."

Opposite meaning: This is confusing, but as a noun, a 'sanction' is an action taken in order to punish or change another's behavior. For example, governments often impose economic sanctions against a nation they feel is behaving badly.

Sentence: In full support of the president, Congress *sanctioned* his use of military force.

SANGUINE (SANG-gwinn) *adj* — **optimistic; cheerful**

Sounds like: sang win

Picture: A young woman is in a singing contest and has just finished her song. She comes backstage and says to her mother, "I know I won. I *sang* more than well enough to *win*. I'm sure of it!"

Other forms: Sanguineness *(noun);* sanguinely *(adv)*

Sentence: Her *sanguine* outlook was contagious, and soon everyone was feeling hopeful.

SARDONIC (sar-DONN-ik) *adj*
— **humorous, but humor tinged with sarcasm or disdain; cynical**

Sounds like: Sardine Nick

Picture: A sardine named Nick who's working as a stand-up comedian. Much of his act consists of sardonic, sarcastic humor.

Other form: Sardonically *(adv)*

Sentence: The movie had a *sardonic* tone that, while funny, was also depressing.

93

SCANTY (SCANT-ee) *adj* — **small in quantity; insufficient**

Looks like: scan tea

Picture: The lady named Emma who gives tea to anyone who comes by (see AMITY). One day, with a few hundred people waiting at her front door, Emma goes to the pantry to get more teabags. She typically has dozens of boxes, but as she scans the tea on the shelves, she realizes that she has very little — certainly not enough for such a large number of uninvited guests. "Oh, dear," she says to herself, "I wonder if any of them drink coffee."

Other forms: Scantily *(adv)*; scantiness *(noun)*; scant *(adj)*

Sentence: With such *scanty* evidence, the prosecution was forced to drop the charges.

SCRUPULOUS (SKROOP-yoo-luss) *adj* — **very thorough; or, doing what is right and ethical**

Sounds like: scoop you loose

Picture: You're lying on the beach, enjoying the last rays of warm sunshine. Everyone else has left, so the beach is deserted except for you and your radio. Out of the corner of your eye, you see a gang of five-year-old children approaching your blanket. There are perhaps nine or ten of them, each armed with a plastic pail and shovel. Several are wearing necklaces made out of what appear to be shark's teeth. You grow a little uneasy, but remind yourself that they're only children. The next thing you know, you've been yanked out of your chair, your hands and feet tied, and you're being buried standing up about ten feet from the water's edge. Five minutes later, up to your lower lip in sand, you watch the gang of children walk off down the beach. You attempt to squirm free but can't move. You check the angle of the sun and try to estimate how much time you have before high tide. As apprehension slowly turns to panic, you notice that one of the children has returned, plastic shovel in hand. "What are you going to do?" you ask nervously. "I'm going to scoop you loose," he answers. "It's the only ethical thing to do." And he begins to dig you out of the sand, carefully, methodically, one tiny scoop at a time.

Other forms: Scrupulousness *(noun)*; scrupulously *(adv)*

Sentence: Rachel was *scrupulous* in her search, thoroughly examining every book on the subject.

SCRUTINIZE (SKROO-tin-ize) *verb* — **examine closely; inspect carefully**

Sounds like: screwed-in eyes

Picture: A "Frankenstein's Monster Look-Alike Contest." The judge is holding a magnifying glass and examining one of several monsters lined up for inspection. "Hmmm," says the judge. "Screwed-in eyes. Minus five points. The eyes should be plug-ins."

Other form: Scrutiny *(noun)*

Sentence: The inspection went on for hours because the captain *scrutinized* every locker.

SECLUSION (seh-KLOO-zhun) *noun* — **separation from other people; isolation**

Sounds like: sick Lucien

Picture: Two people standing outside a closed door. One says to the other, "Lucien is sick and wants to be left alone."

Other form: Secluded *(adj)*

Sentence: After resigning from office, President Nixon went into *seclusion* for many months.

SECTARIAN (sek-TAIR-ee-un) *adj* — **limited to the beliefs of a small group, such as a religious sect; narrow in scope**

Sounds like: secretary Ann

Picture: A secretary, Ann, who belongs to a religious group consisting of other secretaries. On her coffee break, she preaches to co-workers: "I'm not interested in ritual. I'm interested in the religion of secretaries. What kind of correction fluid will lead us to freedom from the bondage of retyping? Where are we to find ultimate truth, in the dictionary or in the spell checker? Is there an afterlife, and if so, what color Post-It Notes do they use there?"

Other form: Sect *(noun)*

Sentence: Terry had big questions, and needed to break free of the *sectarian* views of her childhood.

SEDITIOUS (seh-DISH-uss) *adj* — **trying to stir up a revolt against an authority figure**

Sounds like: said dishes

Picture: The mother is telling her son, for the fourth time, to please wash the dishes ("I said *dishes!*") But the son is being urged by his older sister to refuse: "Tell her you won't do it. If you wash them tonight, she'll just tell you to do them again next week."

Other forms: Sedition *(noun)*; seditiously *(adv)*

Sentence: Before the revolution, many citizens were imprisoned for *seditious* activity.

SENTENTIOUS (sen-TENN-shuss) *adj* — **short and to the point; terse**

Sounds like: send ten shoes

Picture: Mother and father reading a very short letter from their daughter, who is away studying dance. It says, "Love dance school. Send ten shoes."

Other forms: Sententiousness *(noun)*; sententiously *(adv)*

Sentence: The memo was thoughtlessly *sententious*, offering no explanation.

SERPENTINE (SIR-pen-tine) *adj* — **coiled; twisted; winding**

Looks like: serpent   Rhymes with: Turpentine

Picture: A serpent (snake) that has coiled itself around a can of turpentine. The curved shape of the snake's body would be described as serpentine. (Also pronounced SIR-pen-teen.)

Sentence: It would be hard to drive a bus on such a *serpentine* road.

SERVILE (SERV-ile) *adj* — **like a slave; subservient; submissive**

Sounds like: serve aisle

Picture: A man in a movie theater. He gets up to get popcorn, not for himself or his date, but for everyone in their aisle. He buys the snacks and serves them, all the time apologizing for being so slow and inconsiderate.

Other form: Servility *(noun)*

Sentence: He had no authority; his role was a strictly *servile* one.

SKEPTIC (SKEP-tik) *noun* — **one who doesn't believe unless he's shown absolute proof; doubter**

Sounds like: skip tick

Picture: A man is in a museum looking at the world's most accurate watch, housed in a display case. According to the sign, the watch will lose less than a second every million years. The man compares the ticking of this magnificent timepiece with the watch he's wearing on his arm. To his surprise, he finds that the museum watch skips a tick every time the second hand goes around. In other words, it loses a second every minute! He runs to tell the museum director, but the director refuses to believe the story. "Impossible," he says. "That's the most accurate watch ever made. Skip a tick? I refuse to believe it."

Other forms: Skepticism *(noun);* skeptical *(adj);* skeptically *(adv)*

Sentence: They all swore they saw a ghost, but the landlord remained *skeptical.*

SLANDER (SLAN-der) *noun* — **negative oral remarks about another person that are untrue**

Sounds like: slammed her

Picture: Couple watching television talk show. Referring to female guest on the show, one of the viewers says, "She really slammed her! 'Liar. Thief. Killer.' And to think she was talking about her own mother!"

Other forms: Slander *(verb);* slanderous *(adj)*

Sentence: You can't claim *slander* if the statements about you are true.

SOLEMN (SOL-im) *adj* — **serious; somber; grave**

Sounds like: sell 'em

Picture: They used to be wealthy, but no more. They've spent their savings, sold their cars, and rented out their house. Now they're gathering some of their possessions for a tag sale to raise money for food. When the woman holds up her husband's golf clubs, he says sadly, "Sell 'em."

Other forms: Solemnity *(noun);* solemnly *(adv)*

Sentence: A funeral director must be *solemn* and friendly at the same time.

SLOUGH (SLUFF) *verb* — **discard; cast off; shed**

Rhymes with: stuff

Picture: The "Slough and Stuff Clinic," where snakes go to donate their old skin (which they slough off). Other less fortunate snakes come by to be matched up with the old skins and then stuffed into them. (Says one of the sloughers on his way out: "Hey, if the dinosaurs had recycled, who knows?")

Sentence: The old dog *sloughed* off a thick coating of dried mud, then ran into the lake.

SOMBER (SOMM-ber) *adj* — **dark; gloomy**

Looks like: sombrero (Mexican hat)

Picture: A village in Mexico, where happiness and fun are not allowed. Whenever a stranger or visiting family arrives on vacation, the people of the town take out their Somber Sombreros. These magical hats instantly bring forth clouds to cover the sun, and sad feelings to drive away the joy — and the visitors.

Other forms: Somberness *(noun);* somberly *(adv)*

Sentence: The *somber* music told us something unpleasant was about to happen in the movie.

SONOROUS (SAHN-er-uss) *adj*
— **loud, full in sound; booming**

Sounds like: son of Russ

Picture: The same Russ who yells at everyone who works for him (see ONEROUS). Now Russ and his wife have a baby, a boy named Son of Russ, whose voice is unbelievably loud. Russ is on the couch trying to take a nap (Son of Russ kept him up all night). But once again, the baby's booming cry is bounding down the stairs and bouncing off the walls, right into his father's ears.

Other forms: Sonorously *(adv)*; sonorousness *(noun)*

Sentence: The tuba's *sonorous* notes filled the tiny hall with sound.

SPECIOUS (SPEE-shuss) *adj*
— **having a false or misleading appearance; only seeming to be true**

Sounds like: spy shoes

Picture: A spy's apartment. When the enemy spy enters, he doesn't realize the shoes on the floor are really a video camera. They appear to be an ordinary pair of shoes.

Other forms: Speciously*(adv);* speciousness *(noun)*

Sentence: The ad's *specious* claims fooled people into buying something that didn't work.

SPORADIC (spor-ADDIK) *adj*
— **occurring infrequently and without predictability; occasional**

Sounds like: store addict

Picture: A man who is addicted to shopping. He goes to every store he can get to, browsing quickly, sometimes buying, then running out to the next store. (Observer: "Does he come in here often?" Store owner: "Nah. It's sporadic. He has a lot of stores to cover.")

Other form: Sporadically *(adv)*

Sentence: The thunder and rain were *sporadic* and never did turn into a full-blown storm.

SPURIOUS (SPYER-ee-us) *adj*
— **false; fake; misleading**

Looks like: spur furious

Picture: A cowboy is furious about the spurs he just received from a mail order company. The spurs, advertised as "genuine silver-plated iron," turned out to be made of aluminum foil. "I'm furious about these spurs," he says. "These are fake and this is false advertising." Then, after a few seconds he adds, "I'd challenge those mail order people to a showdown, but these impressive-lookin' guns they sold me are made out of cardboard."

Other forms: Spuriously *(adv)*; spuriousness *(noun)*

Sentence: You may be innocent, but *spurious* charges can still cause plenty of damage.

STAGNANT (STAG-nent) *adj*
— **motionless; unchanging; dull**

Looks like: stage ant

Picture: An ant performing on stage. The ants in the audience begin to complain that the actor hasn't moved or said anything for an hour. Says one: "The play is starting to stagnate."

Other forms: Stagnate *(verb);* stagnation *(noun)*

Sentence: *Stagnant* water gives mosquitoes a calm environment in which to thrive.

STATIC (STAT-ik) *adj* — **unchanging; motionless**

Sounds exactly like: static, as in electrical interference

Picture: A woman comes home from work, picks up the telephone, and realizes that the static she'd complained about that morning is still there. "I called the telephone company and they said they were going to get rid of this static. But nothing has changed. The static is still here." (Her son: "Maybe they couldn't understand what you were saying with all that static.")

Other forms: Stasis *(noun);* statically *(adv)*   Sentence: Traffic was *static* for almost an hour.

STEALTH (STELTH) *noun* — **secretive behavior**

Looks like: steal wealth

Picture: A very quiet, highly-skilled burglar breaking into the home of a wealthy person. Everything the burglar does (or doesn't do) in getting into the house without being detected is an example of stealth.

Other forms: Stealthy *(adj);* stealthily *(adv)*

Sentence: A good pickpocket's two major traits are *stealth* and dexterity.

STOIC (STO-ik) *noun* — **a person who shows no response to pleasure or pain; someone who is impassive**

Sounds like: his toe wick

Picture: A man who makes candles by pouring melted wax over his foot. After the wax hardens, he lights his big toe, which acts as the wick. Even with his toe wick burning, he shows no sign of pain!

Other forms: Stoic, stoical *(adj);* stoically *(adv)*

Sentence: Even during torture, he was a *stoic* and never responded.

STYMIE (STY-mee) *verb* — **block; get in the way of; hamper**

Sounds exactly like: Stymie (remember the character on "The Little Rascals"?)

Note: "Stymie" originally referred to a golf situation in which one ball blocked another.

Picture: Stymie (the little boy) playing golf against a professional golfer. Both players have reached the green, and as his opponent is about to putt, Stymie jumps up and runs onto the green between the hole and the other player. "I'm going to block his shot," he says.

Other forms: Stymie *(noun);* stymied *(adj)*

Sentence: The mouse scampered around the maze, but was *stymied* at every turn.

SUBJUGATE (SUB-juh-gate) *verb* — **take over; enslave**

Sounds like: sub jug gate

Picture: Pirates who have switched from ferries (see NEFARIOUS) to submarines. They take over the sub by knocking the crew unconscious with jugs and gates. Then they use the crew as slave labor.

Other form: Subjugation *(noun)*

Sentence: The *subjugation* of one group of people by another is one of the horrors of human nature.

SUBLIME (suh-BLIME) *adj* — **of very special quality; noble**

Looks like: sub lime

Picture: A sub (submarine) shaped like a lime. This sub is so wonderful that it floats in the air above the water.

Other form: Sublimely *(adv)*

Sentence: Her paintings are simple, yet *sublime*.

SUBTLE (SUTT-il) *adj*
— **hard to see or understand; elusive**

Looks like : subtitle

Picture: Man and woman watching a foreign film. As each subtitle appears on the screen, the audience laughs longer and louder. "What?" asks the man. "What's so funny? I just don't get it." Woman: "I think these subtitles are a little too subtle for us."

Other forms: Subtlety *(noun)*; subtly *(adv)*

Sentence: The editor's changes were so *subtle*, even the author didn't notice.

SUCCINCT (suk-SINKT) *adj*
— **short and to the point; concise**

Sounds like : suck sink

Picture: Two teenage boys are standing in the kitchen. One has his face in the sink and he's sucking up gallons of water. His friend turns and explains succinctly to his mother: "Thirsty."

Other forms: Succinctly *(adv)*; succinctness *(noun)*

Sentence: Those five-minute news shows have to be *succinct*.

SUCCOR (SOOK-er) *noun* -- **assistance; relief**

Rhymes with: sugar

Picture: A lady's cat is stuck in a tree. A van pulls up and a bag of sugar comes to the rescue.

Other form: Succor *(verb)*

Sentence: After the fire, rescuers offered *succor* wherever possible.

SUMPTUOUS (SUMP-choo-uss) *adj*
— **rich; magnificent**

Sounds like: some chew us

Picture: A bountiful feast set on a magnificent table. The platters rest on a linen tablecloth. The glasses are expensive crystal, the forks and spoons fine silver. Each plate of food is beautifully prepared and presented. As you approach the feast, you overhear one of the dinner rolls say to a carrot, "People are so impressed when they see us. Some chew us, but most just stand and stare!"

Other forms: Sumptuously *(adv)*; sumptuousness *(noun)*   Note: Does **not** mean delicious.

Sentence: The hotel lobby was so *sumptuous*, I knew instantly I couldn't afford a room.

SUPERFLUOUS (soo-PURR-floo-us) adj
— unnecessary; extra

Sounds like: super floss

Picture: A dental floss that's advertised as "Super Floss," so strong that one strand can lift a fleet of dump trucks without breaking. Such strength, and such claims, would be superfluous — unnecessary, far beyond the possible needs of any customer.

Other forms: Superfluously (adv); superfluity (noun)

Sentence: She had six mailboxes outside her house; five of them were *superfluous*.

SURREPTITIOUS (sir-rupp-TISH-uss) adj
— secretive; furtive; clandestine

Sounds like: syrup tissues

Picture: A spy for a competitive pharmaceutical company has stolen the secret formula for "Coffee Cough Syrup," and is smuggling it out of the building in a box of tissues. (Their slogan, is: "Coffee Cough Syrup, the only cough medicine that keeps you awake while it lets your family get some sleep.")

Other form: Surreptitiously (adv)

Sentence: As an investigative reporter, Al had to be *surreptitious* at times in order to get the facts.

SUSTAIN (suh-STANE) verb — support; nurture; take on

Looks like: Sue Stain

Picture: Sue Stain is the best stain remover in town. Everyone calls Sue whenever they have a stain they can't get out, because she does so much more than just remove stains. Sue offers emotional support, sustaining the family through the ordeal. She provides physical strength, as well, often sustaining the weight of a car while cleaning an oil stain on the driveway. Sue Stain has sustained many injuries while doing her job, yet she has somehow sustained a love for her work.

Other forms: Sustenance (noun); sustaining, sustainable (adj)

Sentence: During times of tragedy, many people are *sustained* by their religious faith.

SYCOPHANT (SIK-oh-fant) noun — someone who flatters in order to gain favor; wimpy follower

Sounds like: sicko fan

Picture: There's this rock star. She is incredibly successful, with hit records coming out every week. She also seems to have more and more fans who follow her wherever she goes. One is the president of her fan club. He writes her letters of praise every day, constantly tells her she's the greatest musician in history, and has even begun to dress like her so that she will like him. But while she appreciates the attention to some degree, she doesn't like or respect this person, and often describes him as "that sicko fan."

Sentence: Some political leaders surround themselves with *sycophants* who just agree with everything.

SYMMETRY (SIMM-uh-tree) noun — balance; having a similar appearance on all sides

Sounds like: similar tree

Picture: A perfect tree, absolutely balanced and in proportion on all sides. For every branch on the left side of the tree, there is a branch of the same length and in the same position on the right side.

Other form: Symmetrical (adj)   Sentence: Rockets need to be *symmetrical* in order to fly.

TACITURN (TASS-it-turn) *adj* — **quiet**

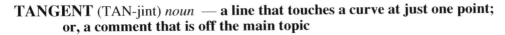

Sounds like: that's Saturn

Picture: The planet Saturn with a face. The rings are across the mouth, so it can't talk.

Other forms: Tacit *(adj);* tacitly *(adv);* taciturnity *(noun)*

Alternate approach: "Taciturnity" sounds like "tax attorney." You might picture a tax attorney working with some clients. No matter what they say, he remains quiet.

Sentence: Anne was worried her *taciturn* boyfriend wouldn't fit in with her talkative family.

TANGENT (TAN-jint) *noun* — **a line that touches a curve at just one point; or, a comment that is off the main topic**

Sounds like: tan gent

Picture: In the winter, the sun's rays are less direct as they approach the earth (in the Northern Hemisphere). Try to imagine the rays as a single straight line and the earth as a curve. Picture those rays just glancing off the earth's surface, meeting the curve at a single point. The rays would be tangent to the earth. That's the first definition. Now let's combine that with the second definition. Picture a man with a deep tan (tan gent) standing on the beach in the middle of winter. You ask him how he got such a tan in the winter, and whether he's been using tanning lotion or going to a tanning salon. He barely addresses your question. Instead of answering, he talks about the angle of the sun's rays and explains that if you prop yourself up just the right way, you can still get a good tan in the winter.

Other forms: Tangential, tangent *(adj)*

Sentence: My uncle would start to tell a story, then go off on a *tangent* and lose me completely.

TANTAMOUNT (TANT-uh-mount) *adj* — **equal; comparable**

Looks like: Tonto mount

Picture: As the Lone Ranger looks on, Tonto mounts his horse by jumping straight up from a standing position. The Lone Ranger is amazed: "Tonto, that mount of yours is tantamount to a ten-foot high jump. You could win a gold medal!" Tonto: "Only one problem. I'd need my horse to stand under the bar."

Sentence: Driving the getaway car is *tantamount* to bank robbery, even if you never enter the bank.

TEMPER (TEM-per) *verb* — **bring into balance; moderate**

Sounds exactly like: temper (as in, he has a bad temper)

Picture: An inventor has created a machine that moderates a person's temper. The angry subject sits next to a panel and places a helmet on his head. The helmet's wires are attached to the panel, and as the inventor adjusts the dials, the participant's mood begins to change; he calms down, becoming more even-tempered.

Other forms: Temper, temperance *(noun);* tempered *(adj)*

Sentence: Frank's excitable nature was *tempered* by Paula's composure.

TENACIOUS (ten-AY-shuss) *adj* — **strong; persistent; determined to hold on**

Sounds like: tennis shoes

Picture: The women's finals at Wimbledon. After the match, the winner sits down to take off her tennis shoes, but she can't. Even with the help of her opponent, the judge, two ball boys, and seventeen spectators pulling at her shoes, they won't come off her feet. (Tennis shoes can be tenacious.)

Other forms: Tenacity *(noun)*; tenaciously *(adv)*

Sentence: The defensive lineman was small but *tenacious*, and he sacked the quarterback twice.

TENTATIVE (TEN-ta-tiv) *adj* — **not fully developed or definitely planned; provisional**

Sounds like: tend to give

Picture: Woman interviewing a man for a job. She is responding to his question about vacation time by saying, "We *tend to give* two weeks' vacation the first year, but that isn't definite yet for this particular job. I'd have to let you know later."

Other forms: Tentatively *(adv)*; tentativeness *(noun)*

Sentence: We made *tentative* plans to go camping, as long as it didn't rain.

TENUOUS (TEN-yoo-uss) *adj* — **thin; flimsy**

Sounds like: ten U.S.

Picture: You're traveling in a country where money is made of neither metal nor paper, but slabs of stone. A native of the country is showing you how his currency is so much more durable than American money. For example, his "ten pound" bill is a 12-inch x 12-inch sheet of slate that actually weighs ten pounds. "In comparison," he says, holding up a paper-thin American ten dollar bill, "this is ten U.S. Pretty thin and flimsy, wouldn't you agree?"

Other forms: Tenuousness *(noun)*; tenuously *(adv)*

Sentence: With the volcano about to erupt, their chances of making it to safety were *tenuous*.

TERSE (TERSE) *adj* — **of few words; to the point; pithy**

Rhymes with: purse
Sounds like: t'sers (a short, concise way of saying, "it's hers")

Picture: A man is walking down the aisle of an airplane, headed for the bathroom. On the way, he trips over a purse, falls headfirst onto someone's lap, and lands face-down in a plate of food he can't recognize even that close. When he manages to pull himself back to a standing position, he's furious. Glaring at the woman seated next to the purse, the man is about to launch into a diatribe when she looks up from her magazine, gestures to the lady across the aisle, and says simply, "T'sers."

Other forms: Terseness *(noun)*; tersely *(adv)*

Sentence: Norman always responded to telemarketers with a terse "No, thank you."

THRIFTY (THRIF-tee) *adj* — **careful about managing money**

Rhymes with: fifty

Picture: A little boy holding a fifty dollar bill and talking to a little girl. "See this fifty?" he asks her. "I've had this since my seventh birthday. Got it from my Uncle Phil. Haven't spent a penny of it in two years. Wanna know why? It's because I'm thrifty. I keep my expenses down. I let my parents pay for my meals, my clothes, and my entertainment. And they don't charge me rent, so I have no overhead."

Other forms: Thriftiness *(noun)*; thriftily *(adv)*

Sentence: Aunt Judy said she bought small presents because she was *thrifty*, but she was just cheap.

TIMOROUS (TIM-er-uss) *adj* — **afraid**

Sounds like: Tim or us

Picture: Group of teenagers outside a large, spooky house. Their friend, Tim, has somehow gotten trapped inside and now they must make a decision about going in to rescue him. "Look," says one frightened boy, "I don't see why we should go in. I think there's a ghost in this house and he's definitely going to get somebody. It's either Tim or us." "Yeah," agrees one of the girls. "Let it be Tim."

Other forms: Timorousness *(noun)*; timorously *(adv)*   Connect with: Timid. But don't confuse "timorous" with "temerity," which means "recklessness."

Sentence: Too *timorous* to go to the door alone, the little boy waited for the other trick-or-treaters.

TIRADE (TY-rade) *noun* — **a long and bitter speech; diatribe**

Sounds like: tie raid

Picture: A man goes to his closet to get his blue tie. It isn't there. He looks for his red tie, the one with the little penguins on it. Gone. He searches for his green and white New York Jets tie. It's missing, too. In fact, there isn't a tie to be found. He storms up to his teenage son's room, flings open the boy's closet door, and finds all of his ties, hanging on a wooden rack. He then launches into a harsh, angry, biting, twenty minute speech about his son's lack of consideration. (Son, after his father has finished: "Does this mean I can't borrow your black sweater tonight?")

Sentence: After the team's ninth straight loss, the coach's *tirade* could be heard in the parking lot.

TORPID (TOR-pid) *adj* — **sluggish; dull; lacking enthusiasm**

Looks like: torpedo

Picture: A torpedo that was launched from a submarine has been traveling for hundreds of miles under the water. It gradually slows down and eventually comes to rest on the ocean floor, exhausted from its long trip. A curious dolphin swims over to see what's going on. "I'm just too tired," says the torpedo. "I can't even remember where I'm supposed to go or what I'm looking for. I think I'm a heat-seeking missile, but with these allergies, who can seek anything? I just want to take a nap."

Other forms: Torpor, torpidity *(nouns)*; torpidly *(adv)*   Note: Insipid, torpid, and vapid all end with "pid" and share the quality of dullness. When you see or hear one, think of the other two. It will help you remember their meanings.

Sentence: Sleep-deprived and depressed, Gary slogged through each day in a *torpid* state.

103

TRANSLUCENT (tranz-LOO-sent) *adj* — **permitting light to pass through**

Sounds like: trains loosened

Picture: Two train cars have uncoupled (loosened). When they move apart, the sun shines between them.

Other forms: Translucence *(noun)*; translucently *(adv)*

Sentence: The windows hadn't been cleaned in years, but now they were *translucent* once again.

TREPIDATION (trep-ih-DAY-shun) *noun* — **fear**

Sounds like: trap a dachshund (a dachshund is a dog with a long body and short legs)

Picture: Several young boys have set a trap for a neighborhood animal. They don't care what they catch, as long as it's breathing and they can tease it before they let it go. Waiting behind a large tree and eating salt-free pretzels, the boys hold the end of a rope whose far end is tied in a noose and hung over a branch. After several anxious minutes, a dachshund that has gotten loose from his yard walks right into the trap and the boys yank him upside down with a sudden and fierce jerk on the rope. Whooping and slapping each other on the back, the young hunters celebrate their achievement. But when they finally turn to begin torturing their victim, the look of terror in his eyes freezes their hands and feet. They are filled with guilt and regret at what they've done to this frightened dog. Carefully lowering him from the tree, they pet and hug him and feed him the last of their salt-free pretzels.

Sentence: Alone in the house at night for the first time, Ed was filled with *trepidation*.

TRITE (TRITE) *adj*
— **overused; common; stale**

Sounds like: trout

Picture: A trout as the teacher in a 'school' of fish. The students are bored with their teacher's constant use of cliches (dull sayings): "Remember, class, there are plenty of other fish in the sea. It's a great big ocean out there. It's sink or swim..."

Other forms: Tritely *(adv)*; triteness *(noun)*

Sentence: Phrases that were once fresh and original now seem *trite* and dull.

YOU LENT YOUR TRUCK TO THAT MANIAC?

TURBULENCE (TUR-byoo-lence) *noun*
— **violent disturbance**

Sounds like: terrible ants

Picture: Enormous ants attack a city. They squash buildings, eat entire Burger Kings, and grab airplanes out of the sky.

TRUCULENT (TRUK-yoo-lent) *adj*
— **aggressive; savage; cruel**

Sounds like: truck you lent

Picture: Two men fleeing from a dump truck that's about to run them down. One of the men lent the truck to the cruel driver.

Other form: Truculence *(noun)*

Sentence: Pirates tend to be somewhat *truculent*.

Other form: Turbulent *(adj)*   Sentence: Except for a little *turbulence*, the plane ride was smooth.

TYRANNY (TEER-uh-nee) *noun*
— **rule based on absolute power or cruelty**

Looks like: Tyrannosaur (the dinosaur)

Picture: A Tyrannosaurus Rex, or any ferocious dinosaur, seated on a throne. "I am the king!" he growls. "I rule everyone! And anybody who doubts that is going to find himself extinct!"

Other form: Tyrant *(noun);* tyrannical *(adj)*

Sentence: The American colonies viewed British rule as *tyranny.*

UBIQUITOUS (yoo-BIK-wit-uss) *adj*
— **existing everywhere at the same time**

Sounds like: a Bic with us

Picture: You're orbiting the Earth in the space shuttle. As you fly over each country, you see millions of people waving their hands in the air. You look more closely and see that every person is holding a Bic cigarette lighter. Then the President calls you on the telephone to explain: "We wanted you to see lights everywhere you go, so we all have a Bic with us."

Other forms: Ubiquity, ubiquitousness *(nouns);* ubiquitously *(adv)*

Sentence: Certain signs of our culture seem to be *ubiquitous,* and are hard to escape.

UNANIMOUS (yoo-NAN-ih-muss) *adj*
— **in total agreement**

Sounds like: you, Nanny Moose

Picture: Nanny Moose (see MAGNANIMOUS) is running for president of the PTA. After the election, the members stand up and announce, "We *all* voted for you, Nanny Moose!"

Other forms: Unanimously *(adv);* unanimity *(noun)*

Note: "Un" means "one" and "animous" means "mind or soul." So unanimous means "of one mind."

Sentence: Everyone wanted Michelle to be class president, so the vote was *unanimous.*

UNDERMINE (UNN-der-mine) *verb*
— **to weaken by wearing away the foundation; to sabotage**

Looks exactly like: under mine

Picture: A diamond mine, discovered and developed by a very hard-working woman. Secretly, the woman's jealous sister has been digging a tunnel under the mine in an effort to weaken its foundation and destroy the operation.

Sentence: Carol tried to *undermine* Don's authority by starting a rumor about him.

UNDULATE (UN-joo-late) *verb*
— **move in a wavy manner**

Sounds like: under lake

Picture: The Loch Ness monster, or some other sea serpent, moving quietly through the dark waters under the lake. Seen from the side, the monster's body moves in waves under the water.

Other forms: Undulated *(adj);* undulation *(noun)*

Sentence: The wind shaped the sand dune into an *undulating* sculpture.

UNERRING (un-EHR-ing) *adj*
— **without making a mistake**

Sounds like: an earring

Picture: A woman wearing a pair of very beautiful earrings. Two other women look at her and one says to the other, "She never fails to wear the right earrings."

Other form: Unerringly *(adv)*

Sentence: The gymnast won the gold medal because he was *unerring* in performing his program.

UNIFORM (YOON-ih-form) *adj*
— **similar; consistent**

Sounds exactly like: uniform

Picture: A Girl Scout troop marching in a parade. One girl says, "Look at us. We're all dressed alike. Same skirts, same socks, same hats..." The other girl responds, "That's why they call them *uniforms*."

Other forms: Uniformity *(noun)*; uniformly *(adv)*

Sentence: Power tools are helpful when you need to cut a lot of lumber into *uniform* lengths.

UNKEMPT (un-KEMPT) *adj*
— **messy; sloppy**

Sounds like: encamped, or in camp

Picture: Two girls at a camp-out, seated in front of their tent. Their clothes are rumpled and dirty, their hair is uncombed.

Sentence: We could tell by his *unkempt* appearance that he hadn't been home in days.

UNPRECEDENTED
(un-PRESS-ih-dent-ed) *adj* — **the first of its kind**

Sounds like: un-presidented

Picture: George Washington's inauguration. It was an unprecedented event, because he was the first president.

Connect with: Precede *(verb)*.

Think of "legal precedent."

Sentence: Sandra Day O'Connor's appointment to the Supreme Court in 1981 was *unprecedented*.

UPBRAID (up-BRADE) *verb*
— **criticize severely; scold**

Looks like: up braid

Picture: A schoolgirl with braided hair. She's being scolded so harshly by the teacher that her braids are standing straight up.

Sentence: He was afraid he would be *upbraided* for his mistake.

USURP (yoo-SERP) *verb*
— **to seize or take over by force**

Sounds like: you slurp

Picture: Two women seated at the counter in a diner. One woman is slurping her soup. The other woman grabs the spoon from her and says, "You slurp and I take your spoon!"

Other form: Usurpation *(noun)*

Sentence: The army violently *usurped* the throne.

USURY (YOO-zhur-ee) *noun* — **the practice of charging a very high rate of interest on loans**

Sounds like: Use Yuri. Also sounds like "usually."

Picture: A man named Yuri who lends money at high interest rates. His slogan is, "If you can afford the highest rates, Use Yuri. Otherwise, get lost." A customer reading his loan contract asks Yuri, "Do you always charge 40% interest?" Yuri answers, "Usually."

Other forms: Usurious *(adj);* usuriously *(adv)*

Sentence: The interest rates on some credit cards are so high, they border on *usury*.

VACILLATE (VASS-ill-ate) *verb* — **move back and forth between choices, unable to decide**

Sounds like: vessel late

Picture: Christopher Columbus trying to decide whether to turn left or right on his way to the new world. "Go left," he says. "No, wait. Turn right. No, left..." (One of his crew says: "Chris, no pressure, but your indecision is making this vessel late, and we promised the Queen we'd get there by 1492.")

Other form: Vacillation *(noun)*

Sentence: Ted *vacillated* so long about what to order that the restaurant closed.

VACUOUS (VAK-yoo-us) *adj* — **empty; stupid; purposeless**

Sounds like: vacuum us

Picture: A woman is vacuuming her large living room. Over in one corner of the room sit three bathtubs (her husband collects them). They're empty, stupid, and have no real purpose. But over the sound of the machine she can hear all three of the bathtubs yelling, "Over here! Please! Vacuum us!"

Other forms: Vacuousness, vacuity *(nouns);* vacuously *(adv)*

Sentence: Barbara's *vacuous* comments irritated the teacher because they wasted time.

VAGRANT (VAY-grent) *noun* — **homeless person; wanderer**

Looks like: VA Grant (VA is the abbreviation for Virginia)

Picture: A man named Grant, wearing tattered clothes and carrying his belongings in a plastic bag, answers a policeman's questions about his current residence:

"So your name is Grant?"
"Yes, sir, Officer."
"Where do you live, Mr. Grant?"
"In VA."
"VA?"
"Virginia. They call me VA Grant. My home is Virginia."
"Any particular place in Virginia?"
"Nope. It's a big state and I use all of it."

Other forms: Vagrant *(adj);* vagrantly *(adv);* vagrancy *(noun)*

Sentence: He had the soul of a *vagrant* and loved to wander from place to place.

VALEDICTORY (val-uh-DIK-ter-ee) *noun* — a farewell speech

Related to: valedictorian (the person with the highest average in a graduating class)

Picture: A high school graduating class. The valedictorian is giving her speech: "My fellow students," she says. "Bye-bye. Farewell. So long. See ya. Until we meet again..." (One student to another: "I hate long goodbyes.")

Other forms: Valediction, valedictorian *(nouns)*

Sentence: The general's *valedictory* to his departing troops was an emotional one.

VALIDATE (VAL-ih-date) *verb* — confirm; corroborate; support; sanction

Sounds like: valid date

Picture: Two archeologists. One is handing the other a small statue and saying, "I've done all the tests on this piece and believe it was made in 1955 B.C. It was a Thursday, June 16th. Will you please confirm that this is a valid date?"

Other forms: Valid *(adj);* validity, validation *(nouns)*

Sentence: Ellen felt *validated* when the company took a chance and supported her idea.

VAPID (VAH-pid) *adj* — dull; boring; lacking flavor or spark

Looks like: vapor

Picture: A woman is visiting a country called Vaporland. She sits with a group of boring natives as they explain their culture to her. "You see," says the leader, "everything here centers around vapor. We eat and drink only vapor. Our artwork depicts only vapor. We talk and think only about vapor. And the more dull the vapor, the more wonderful it makes us feel."

Other forms: Vapidity, vapidness *(nouns);* vapidly *(adv)*

Sentence: The show was trite and *vapid*, so naturally it was a big hit.

VERACITY (ver-RASS-sih-tee) *noun* — truth

Looks like: Vera City

Picture: Vera City, where everyone always tells the truth.

Other form: Veracious *(adj)*

Connect with: Verify

Sentence: The skeptical detective doubted the *veracity* of the suspect's alibi.

VERBOSE (ver-BOSE) *adj* — very talkative; loquacious

Sounds like: verb hose

Picture: A man watering his flowers with a garden hose. A steady stream of words is coming from his mouth, and from the hose!

Other forms: Verboseness, verbosity *(nouns)*

Sentence: The *verbose* woman at the next table was giving us a headache.

VERSATILE (VERS-uh-tile) *adj* — **having many talents or uses**

Sounds like: reverse a tile

Picture: A TV commercial promoting Revers-a-Tile, "the amazing new floor tile with 1001 uses. Each Revers-a-Tile is a ceramic tile. Flip it over and it's a square of carpet. Flip it again and it's a square of artificial grass. Revers-a-Tile covers floors, walls, counter tops, ceilings, and driveways. It's also great for quilts, bathtubs, roofs, and highway overpasses."

Other form: Versatility *(noun)*

Sentence: Most small companies value *versatility* -- they can't afford a different person for every task.

THE WOOL VEST IS GONE, BUT THE ITCH IS STILL HERE!

VESTIGE (VESS-tij) *noun* — **something left behind; evidence of something that has vanished**

Sounds like: vest itch

Picture: A man suffering from the itch left behind by his wool vest.

Other form: Vestigial *(adj)*

Sentence: The last *vestiges* of winter melted away today.

VILIFY (VILL-ih-fie) *verb* — **defame; attack someone's reputation**

Sounds like: village fly

Picture: A giant fly, known as the Village Fly, who goes from house to house, saying bad things about the neighbors.

Other form: Vilification *(noun)*

Sentence: He was so *vilified* in the press that his reputation never recovered.

VIRULENT (VEER-uh-lent) *adj* — **poisonous or destructive; filled with hate or anger; harsh**

Sounds like: Vera lint

Picture: Vera is filled with hate. So poisonous is her personality that even the lint from her clothing causes people to get sick.

Other forms: Virulence *(noun);* virulently *(adv)*

Sentence: An extremely *virulent* strain of flu virus swept across the country.

VISCOUS (VISS-kuss) *adj* — **resistant to flow, like a very thick liquid; or, sticky**

Sounds like: biscuits

This is a somewhat confusing word, with two different meanings. But here's a way to remember both of them. Picture a pipe filled with biscuits that are half-baked. The biscuits are really a thick, sticky batter that doesn't flow through the pipe very well.

Other form: Viscosity *(noun)*.

Sentence: High-*viscosity* oil is used to protect engines.

VOLATILE (VAHL-ah-till) *adj* — **capable of evaporating, exploding, or changing moods quickly**

Sounds like: volley tile

Picture: A game similar to volleyball, except that instead of a ball, a tile is hit back and forth over the net. The tile is volatile and could explode at any time, so the players try to keep it in the air.

Other form: Volatility *(noun)*

Sentence: The judge had a *volatile* temper, so the lawyers were on their best behavior.

VOLUBLE (VOL-yoo-bull) *adj* — **comfortable with speech; always ready to talk**

Sounds like: valuable

Picture: A glass case, filled with valuables, in a jewelry store late at night. The diamond pendant never stops talking. A watch says to a friendship ring nearby, "There she goes again! Doesn't she ever get tired? If I could just get my hands on a choker..."

Other forms: Volubility *(noun);* volubly *(adv)*

Sentence: A politician must have a *voluble* personality, especially when campaigning.

WAIVE (WAVE) *verb* — **to voluntarily abandon a legal right; relinquish; postpone**

Sounds exactly like: wave

Picture: Policeman saying, "You have the right to remain silent. If you wish to give up that right, wave your hand and start talking."

Other form: Waiver *(noun)*

Sentence: Lew *waived* his right to an attorney and defended himself.

WANE (WAIN) *verb* — **grow smaller**

Sounds like: the name "Wayne"

Picture: Wayne is getting shorter, and his clothes are becoming too big for him.

Connect with: Wax *(verb)*

Sentence: With her strength *waning*, she grabbed the rope just in time.

WANTON (WAHN-tun) *adj* — **excessive; uncontrolled; lustful**

Looks like: wonton (as in wonton soup)

Picture: The groom at the wedding has eaten too much wonton soup (it makes him behave as if he were drunk). Now he's wearing his bride's veil and dancing with three women at the same time. (His wife: "I knew we should've gone with the split pea.")

Other form: Wantonness *(noun)*

Sentence: His *wanton* behavior was widely condemned.

WARRANTED (WAR-ent-ed) *adj* — **justified; authorized**

Looks like: Warren Ted

Picture: Warren Ted is the town bully. He's just punched a smaller man in the nose and is walking away. The victim, lying on the ground and holding his face, says to the woman with him, "That wasn't warranted." The woman looks over at Warren Ted and says, "Yes it was. I'd recognize him anywhere."

Other forms: Warrant *(noun);* warrant *(verb)*

Sentence: Despite the coach's protests, the referees agreed that the penalty was *warranted.*

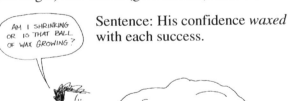

WASTREL (WASE-tril) *noun* — **person who wastes his money or resources**

Sounds like: waste trail

Picture: A man who has put all of his money into a backpack and set out to hike across the country. Somewhere in the woods, his money begins to fall from the backpack. As he continues to walk, unaware of the problem, he leaves behind a trail of wasted money. (Says one chipmunk to another: "He's just a wastrel on the Waste Trail of life.")

Sentence: A *wastrel* shouldn't complain about what he's lost.

WAX (WACKS) *verb* — **grow gradually larger**

Sounds exactly like: wax

Picture: Wayne (see WANE) standing next to a ball of wax that seems to be getting larger.

Connect with: Wane *(verb)*. The moon waxes (gets larger) and wanes (gets smaller) each month.

AM I SHRINKING OR IS THAT BALL OF WAX GROWING?

Sentence: His confidence *waxed* with each success.

WITHER (WIH-ther) *verb* — **dry or shrivel up; lose life or energy**

Sounds like: with her

Picture: A woman who carries old, shriveled flowers *with her* wherever she goes.

Other form: Withered *(adj)*

Sentence: He *withered* in the hot desert sun.

WIZENED (WIZZ-ind) *adj* — **old and wrinkled; withered**

Sounds like: Wiz end

Picture: The Wizard of Oz as a very, very old man (near the end of his life). He looks wrinkled and withered (but he still has enough strength and energy left to sing "If I Only Had Some Teeth").

Sentence: Her face was *wizened*, not from age, but from her experiences.

111

XENOPHOBIA (ZEN-uh-foe-bee-uh) *noun* — **the fear or hatred of anything foreign**

Picture: A crowd of Earthlings running in fear from an alien creature and his spaceship. "Run!" they scream. "He's from the planet Xenon!"

Other form: Xenophobic *(adj)*

Sentence: Millions of people have been killed because of nothing more than *xenophobia*.

YIELD (YEELD) *verb* — **give up; give in**

Sounds exactly like: yield

Think of: A yield sign. When you come to a yield sign, you give in to the other driver; you surrender the right of way. So picture a man holding a yield sign and giving it to the woman standing next to him.

Sentence: We *yielded* to their pleas and went to the party.

YOKE (YOKE) *verb* — **to link, or join together; marry**

Sounds exactly like: yolk

Picture: Two chicken farmers getting married. The man takes out a ring made of egg yolk and slides it on the woman's finger. "Now," he says, "we are yoked together forever."

Other form: Yoke *(noun)* — the wooden frame used to join two oxen so they can pull the plow.

Sentence: Walter was *yoked* to his job and his family had to settle for second place.

ZEALOT (ZELL-ut) *noun* — **person with an extreme enthusiasm for a belief or activity; fanatic**

Sounds like: sell it

Picture: A used-car salesman who is driven to sell as many cars as he can. His motto is "Sell it!" His zealous behavior is both admired and criticized by his co-workers. One day his zeal is curbed, at least momentarily, by one of his fellow salesmen, who rushes over to him and says, "What do you mean, 'Sell it'? That's *my* car!"

Other forms: Zeal, zealotry, zealousness *(nouns);* zealous *(adj);* zealously *(adv)*

Sentence: Many religious *zealots* have been willing to die for their beliefs.

ZENITH (ZEE-nith) *noun* — **the highest point; apex**

Sounds exactly like: Zenith (as in Zenith television sets)

Picture: King Kong climbing the Empire State Building (see APEX). When he gets to the top, he throws away the X, replacing it with a Zenith television. The TV is now at the highest point.

Sentence: She retired at the *zenith* of her career, before her skills began to decline.

135 more

Here are another 135 words that I might have included in the main part of the book, but didn't. There were three possible reasons for excluding these words. (1) I may have thought enough people would already know the word. (2) I couldn't come up with an appropriate picture for the word. (3) I ran out of room. Whatever the reasons, these words are important for you to know. Some of them may very well appear on your SAT.

Admonish *(verb)* — to warn or scold, but in a caring way
Adversary *(noun)* — opponent; enemy
Aesthetic *(adj)* — appealing to the senses; beautiful
Animosity *(noun)* — a feeling of resentment, hostility, or enmity
Apprehension *(noun)* — nervousness; fear
Authoritarian *(adj)* — having complete control over many people
Autonomous *(adj)* — having the freedom of self-government; free
Blasphemy *(noun)* — disrespect toward God or something sacred
Blithe *(adj)* — merry; carefree
Comprehensive *(adj)* — covering completely; having broad scope
Conciliatory *(adj)* — agreeable; friendly; appeasing
Debilitate *(verb)* — to weaken
Delineate *(verb)* — to explain or describe in detail
Depravity *(noun)* — corruption; perversion; evil
Detached *(adj)* — separate; indifferent; aloof
Deterrent *(noun)* — something that prevents or discourages an act
Devious *(adj)* — tricky; crooked
Didactic *(adj)* — intended to teach; informative; instructional
Diligence *(noun)* — hard work; perseverance
Diminution *(noun)* — the act of decreasing
Discriminating *(adj)* — selecting carefully; judicious
Disinclination *(noun)* — tending to avoid; aversion
Dispassionate *(adj)* — not emotionally involved; objective
Disputatious *(adj)* — tending to argue; or, controversial
Disseminate *(verb)* — to spread or give out; to disburse
Dissonance *(noun)* — clashing sounds; lack of agreement
Document *(verb)* — to provide evidence; to back up with facts
Dubious *(adj)* — doubtful; questionable
Duplicity *(noun)* — sneakiness; contradiction; deceit
Elaborate *(verb)* — expand an explanation to include more details
Elusive *(adj)* — hard to catch or understand; evasive
Emaciated *(adj)* — extremely thin; wasted away
Embryonic *(adj)* — at an early stage of development
Engender *(verb)* — cause to exist; produce
Epic *(adj)* — large in scope or size
Equanimity *(noun)* — calmness; composure
Equivocal *(adj)* — misleading; uncertain
Erroneous *(adj)* — in error; false; mistaken
Execute *(verb)* — do what is requested; carry out

Exemplary *(adj)* — deserving imitation; serving as an example

Exemplify *(verb)* — show by example

Exhaustive *(adj)* — complete; thorough

Exonerate *(verb)* — to free from blame; to exculpate

Expedient *(adj)* — useful for reaching a desired end

Explicit *(adj)* — absolutely clear; free from ambiguity

Facilitate (verb) — make easier

Fanaticism *(noun)* — excessive, irrational enthusiasm

Fluctuate *(verb)* — to go up and down or back and forth

Frivolity *(noun)* — silliness; lack of seriousness

Gesticulate *(verb)* — to gesture dramatically when speaking

Glib *(adj)* — smooth-talking; slick

Grandiose *(adj)* — large; grand; filled with splendor

Gratuitous *(adj)* — free of charge; or, uncalled for and unwarranted

Haughty *(adj)* — proud to the point of being arrogant

Hedonism *(noun)* — the belief that only pleasure is worth pursuing

Hypothetical *(adj)* — not necessarily real; based upon supposition

Implement *(verb)* — to put into effect; to carry out

Implication *(noun)* — necessary result of an action; connection

Implicit *(adj)* — understood without explanation; or, inherent

Impugn *(verb)* — to attack with words; to accuse of being false

Impunity *(noun)* — freedom from punishment or harm

Incidental *(adj)* — happening by chance or luck; accidental

Incisive *(adj)* — direct; clear-cut; right to the point

Inclusive *(adj)* — covering or including everything

Incontrovertible *(adj)* — cannot be questioned or doubted

Indefatigable *(adj)* — having endless energy; tireless

Indifferent *(adj)* — impartial; unbiased; apathetic

Indiscriminate *(adj)* — without careful consideration; haphazard

Indulgent *(adj)* — giving in; yielding; lenient

Inherent *(adj)* — having a certain quality by nature; intrinsic

Insidious *(adj)* — gradually harmful; seductive

Instigate *(verb)* — to cause to act; urge; incite

Insuperable *(adj)* — incapable of being dominated or defeated

Intangible *(adj)* — not capable of being touched or perceived

Integrity *(noun)* — solidness of construction or morality; honesty

Interlocutor *(noun)* — someone who participates in a conversation

Interminable *(adj)* — endless

Methodical *(adj)* — step-by-step; sequential; systematic

Modicum *(noun)* — a very small amount

Nascent *(adj)* — recently born or created

Nebulous *(adj)* — unclear; vague

Notoriety *(noun)* — fame, usually obtained by doing something bad

Objective *(adj)* — without prejudice or bias; impartial; fair

Oblivion (noun) — the state of being forgotten

        Oblivious *(adj)* — unaware; forgetful

        Obtrusive *(adj)* — sticking out; or, pushy

Omniscient *(adj)* — knowing everything

Opalescent *(adj)* — reflecting a rainbow of color; dazzling

Ostentatious *(adj)* — overdone to the point of showing off; gaudy

Parochial *(adj)* — having a narrow view; restricted; local

Pedantic *(adj)* — obsessed with the details of knowledge; book-smart

Perturbation *(noun)* — disturbance

Philanthropy *(noun)* — charitable work; generosity

Plethora *(noun)* — over-abundance; excess

Poignancy *(noun)* — something that touches the emotions deeply

Pragmatic *(adj)* — practical

Presumptuous *(adj)* — going too far; overstepping the limits

Prevarication *(noun)* — a lie; mendacity

Proliferation *(noun)* — fast growth

Prolific *(adj)* — productive; fertile

Provincial *(adj)* — limited or restricted; parochial

Quiescent *(adj)* — calm; inactive; latent

Quintessential *(adj)* — being the best or purest example of something

Quixotic *(adj)* — idealistic; impractical (from Don Quixote)

Rebuke *(verb)* — criticize; reprimand; reprove

Rectify *(verb)* — to fix; to correct

Refute *(verb)* — prove wrong by showing evidence; deny

Renounce *(verb)* — to reject past beliefs or actions; repudiate

Reprehensible *(adj)* — deserving of criticism; culpable

Rescind *(verb)* — take back; remove; void

Retract *(verb)* — withdraw; take back a previous statement; recant

Sagacity *(noun)* — wisdom; shrewdness

Satire *(noun)* — a sarcastically humorous depiction

Saturate *(verb)* — fully satisfy; fill to capacity; soak

Savory *(adj)* — pleasing, either to the senses or the mind

Sedulous *(adj)* — hard-working and careful of details; diligent

Spendthrift *(noun)* — someone who wastes money (who is prodigal)

Stalwart *(adj)* — strong; unwavering

Stanch *(verb)* — to stop the flow of (blood, for example)

Staunch *(adj)* — standing firm; solidly loyal

Steadfast *(adj)* — not movable; strong in belief; staunch

Strident *(adj)* — harsh sounding

Stupefy *(verb)* — to cause someone to be groggy or confused

Submissive *(adj)* — tame; subservient; obsequious

Surpass *(verb)* — to go beyond; exceed

Tedious *(adj)* — long and drawn-out; tiresome; boring

Vagary *(noun)* — an unpredictable result or action

Vehement *(adj)* — strongly expressed; powerful

Venerate *(verb)* — respect greatly; revere

Viable *(adj)* — capable of living or functioning

Virtuoso *(noun)* — a highly-skilled person

Vociferous *(adj)* — loud and insistent; vehement; obstreperous

Vulnerable *(adj)* — able to be hurt

Whimsical *(adj)* — unpredictable; capricious

SAT Critical Reading: How to Avoid the Traps

You need a new attitude

For most of your test-taking career, you have been given exams made up by teachers who were on your side. They had taught you the material, and wanted you to prove they did a good job of it. So they were pulling for you to do well.

This may come as a surprise to you, but the people who create and administer the SAT don't especially want you to do well. At least not on their test. The SAT is designed to identify those students who are most likely to succeed in college. So if everyone did well on the SAT, the test would be useless.

Given that shocking bit of news, you must now arm yourself with a weapon you may have never before taken into the test-taking arena. It's called: thinking.

Now don't go getting your feelings hurt, or having bad thoughts about me and members of my family. I know you've done a lot of thinking on tests, and probably also during some other activities. But I'm talking about real, look 'em over extra good, how-are-they-trying-to-rip-me-off-this-time thinking. I'm talking about being smart when some very sneaky people are trying to make you look dumb. I'm talking about being *suspicious*.

I'm also talking about knowing your stuff. Excelling on the SAT involves two things: the right attitude and the right knowledge. Go in without either one and you're going to get devoured, number-2 pencil and all.

How do the SAT testmakers try to trap you on the critical reading part?

Mostly with vocabulary. This part of the SAT tests your ability to understand words and ideas. The testmakers (and colleges) want to see how familiar you are with the language. It's really as simple as that. It's also as complicated as that, because unfortunately, the language we're talking about here is English.

The fact that English may be your native language is quite irrelevant. English is filled, brimming, overflowing with areas of confusion. But because you haven't had to deal with them all at once, they haven't really posed much of a problem. Until now.

As you are no doubt beginning to suspect, the creators of the SAT have combed the English language for every possible source of trouble. And they've skillfully incorporated them into the very essence of the test. Here are a few of the most common:

1. Words that look alike but have different, sometimes opposite, meanings
2. Words that share roots with other words, but mean different things
3. Words that have a common and a less-common meaning
4. Words that have different meanings depending on how they're used
5. Words you know, but don't know you know
6. Words you think you know, but really don't
7. Strange words you may never see again after the SAT

And on and on. Need some real-life examples? Try these:

1. Words that look alike but have different, sometimes opposite, meanings

The word *condemn* means to harshly criticize. The word *condone* means to approve of. See the problem there? People confuse these two words all the time. The friendly folks at SAT-land know that. Which is why they like to use pairs of words like condemn and condone. One of the words will be in the question, and the meaning of the other will appear in the answer. Watch out!

2. Words that share roots with other words, but mean different things

We have all heard about Latin and Greek roots in many English words, and we were taught to connect those words in our minds. Most often this is a helpful thing to do. But once in a while it can create confusion. For example, the word *indolent* means lazy. On the other hand, *redolent* means fragrant. And, if you have one more hand, *doleful* means sad. Since each seems to have the root -*dole*, you might think the words are related. But as you can see from the definitions, there is much opportunity for the SAT to trap you.

3. Words that have a common and a less-common meaning

As a noun, the word *check* has several familiar meanings. It has a familiar meaning as a verb -- to inspect. But it also means to block (a body check in hockey, for example). The word champion may bring to mind a Super Bowl or World Series winner. But as a verb, to champion means to support -- as in "He championed the cause of animal rights." Other examples include: air, temper, trigger, hamper, founder, splinter, document, and wax. All have common and less-common meanings. On the SAT, expect the uncommon.

4. Words that have different meanings depending on how they're used

Sometimes the English language can be mildly bewildering. Sometimes it can be absolutely exasperating. Take, for example, the word *sanction*. As a verb, it means to approve, or give consent. I sanction your actions when I like what you're doing. However, as a noun, the word means the opposite. If the United States doesn't like North Korea's actions, the U.S. might issue economic sanctions against that nation. So sanction as a noun can mean an expression of disapproval or even punishment. (Hey, it's your language.)

5. Words you know, but don't know you know

Once you've learned the word *opaque*, it becomes a familiar word. It has that letter "q" in the middle, and there just aren't that many words like that. So you know *opaque*, as an adjective. But on the SAT, you might see *opaque* as a noun: *opacity*. The "q" is gone. Will you recognize it?

6. Words you think you know, but really don't

You sort of know what *casual* means. You may not be able to put it into a distinct definition, but you can figure out the answer to a question involving this word. The SAT likes to use the word *causal*. Different word, different meaning. Did you catch it? It's easy to miss, because we don't proofread every word we read. We recognize many words by how they look. Unfortunately for you, the words *casual* and *causal* look very much alike. And on the SAT, that can mean only one thing: confusion. Here are a couple more examples. What do you think *quiescent* means? How about *noisome*? Look them up -- you may be surprised.

7. Strange words you may never see again after the SAT

Do you know what *necromancy* means? It refers to an activity involving communication with the dead. You might not expect to see it on the SAT. I've seen it on quite a few. How about *coven*? It means a group of witches. *Dross*? The impurities in metal. *Palisade*? A row of stakes. These are not common words in adult language, so why would the SAT people want you to know them? The simple answer is, they're hoping you don't.

A final point

Please remember, for every example you see here, there are dozens more I've seen on SATs. You'll see them, too, if you do enough practice tests. Eventually you will learn to recognize each kind of trap, even if you haven't seen every example of it before. And you'll be that much closer to your goal, because you will have learned how the testmakers think -- and how you must think.

Is there any guarantee the words in this book will appear on your test? No, only that some of them will. The problem is, we don't know which ones. But every new word you learn improves your odds by some fraction of a percent. So absorb these words, and others, wherever you can. And use them. Because even if you don't see *paucity*, *penchant*, or *perfunctory* on the SAT, knowing them will enrich your life just a little bit.

I hope this book has done the same.

Don't be fooled!

Here's a sampling of the word pairs and groups employed by the SAT to confuse and confound your brain. This list is far from complete, but it will give you an idea of the kinds of words to watch out for.

These have different (sometimes opposite) meanings:

apprehend *and* apprehensive
comprehend *and* comprehensive
condone *and* condemn
ingenious *and* ingenuous
arid *and* arable
casual *and* causal
loath *and* loathe
collaborate *and* corroborate
parity *and* parody
indignant, indigenous, *and* indigent
prescribe *and* proscribe
disperse *and* disburse
doleful, redolent, *and* indolent
censure *and* censor
chasten *and* chaste
pity *and* piety
erratic *and* erotic
decadent *and* decade
quiescent *and* quiet
noisome *and* noisy
disparage *and* disparate
prodigy, prodigal, *and* prodigious
timorous *and* temerity
enervate *and* energize
arcane *and* archaic
thrift *and* spendthrift
compliment *and* complement
wary *and* weary
persecute *and* prosecute
ambiguous *and* ambivalent
voluble *and* valuable
dissemble *and* disassemble
impudent *and* impotent
invidious *and* insidious
proceed *and* precede
conceited *and* conceded
dissent *and* descent
profound *and* profane
innate *and* inane

*These mean a **group** of something:*

coven (witches)
pride (lions)
phalanx (soldiers)
troupe (performers)

*These mean **talkative**:*

garrulous
loquacious
verbose
voluble

*These mean **quiet**:*

laconic
reticent
taciturn
terse

*These mean **scold or criticize**:*

admonish   disparage
castigate   rebuke
censure   reprove
chasten   upbraid
chastise

*These mean **praise**:*

acclaim
accolade
extol
laud
lionize

*These are just **weird words** you have to know for the SAT:*

dross (impurities)
slag (impurities)
charlatan (faker)
necromancy (communication with the dead)
sorcerer (someone who communicates with the dead)
conflagration (big fire)
palisade (row of stakes)

Made in the USA
Lexington, KY
09 December 2011